James Casebere Andreas Gursky Mark Power Hannah Starkey Deborah Baker
Lesley Shearer John Askew John Stezaker Josef Koudelka Jon Thompson Melanie Manchot
David Bate David Chandler Piers Masterson David Alan Mellor Stella Santacatterina
Amanda Hopkinson John Stathatos Joanna Lowry Mark Durden Simon Morrissey Paul Ryan

James Casebere *Two Bunk Cell (cover)*
Toppled Desks (opposite)

portfolio

the catalogue of contemporary
photography in britain

introduction

Hannah Starkey *Untitled*, May 1997

This issue of PORTFOLIO features some of the most innovative photographic art being created and exhibited in the UK in 1999. The architecture of institutions is the source of work by **James Casebere**, **Andreas Gursky** and **Mark Power** (who has been documenting the building of the Millennium Dome in London since early 1998). We are delighted to present **John Stezaker**'s uncanny digital photographs of children, **Hannah Starkey** and **Lesley Shearer**'s staged photographs of young women, commissioned panoramic photographs of Wales by **Josef Koudelka**, **Melanie Manchot**'s large-scale photographic portraits on canvas, **Deborah Baker**'s series of video capture images, **John Askew**'s photographs of Russia, and the performance art of **Jon Thompson**.

plates

Andreas Gursky *San Francisco*

Deborah Baker *Gaze: The Anxious Sign*

number 29 June 1999

Published in June and December by Portfolio Gallery Photography Workshop (Edinburgh) Limited
43 Candlemaker Row, Edinburgh EH1 2QB, UK
Tel (44) 0131 220 1911
Fax (44) 0131 226 4287

Email portfolio@ednet.co.uk
WWW http://www.ednet.co.uk/~portfolio

subscriptions

United Kingdom
Individuals £30 for 4 issues / £17 for 2 issues
Institutions, Libraries and Colleges £45 for 4 issues / £25 for 2 issues
Europe £45 for 4 issues / £25 for 2 issues
Worldwide Air £55 for 4 issues / £30 for 2 issues

distribution

UK Museum and Gallery Bookshops:
PORTFOLIO, 43 Candlemaker Row,
Edinburgh EH1 2QB, UK
Tel (44) 0131 220 1911 Fax (44) 0131 226 4287

retail
Art Data, 12 Bell Industrial Estate,
50 Cunnington Street, London W4 5HB
Tel (44) 0181 747 1061
Fax (44) 0181 742 2319

essays

reviews

Lesley Shearer *Women and Men*

Mark Power *The Millennium Dome, 19 May 1998*

John Stezaker *Angel*

Editor **Gloria Chalmers**

Editorial Assistants **Sophie Allen, Catherine Williams, Elizabeth Pardoe**

Subscriptions and Sales **Lesley Young**

Design Consultants **Tayburn Corporate**

Typesetting **Patricia Bartie**

Set in Foundry Sans **The Foundry**, London

ISSN 1354-4446

Printed on Consort Royal Satin manufactured by Donside Paper Company, Aberdeen

Reprographics by Leeds Photo Litho

Printed by Jackson-Wilson Printers, Leeds

THE SCOTTISH ARTS COUNCIL

Funded by THE ARTS COUNCIL OF ENGLAND

·EDINBVRGH·
THE CITY OF EDINBURGH COUNCIL

James Casebere

Toilets

Two Bunk Cell *(opposite)*

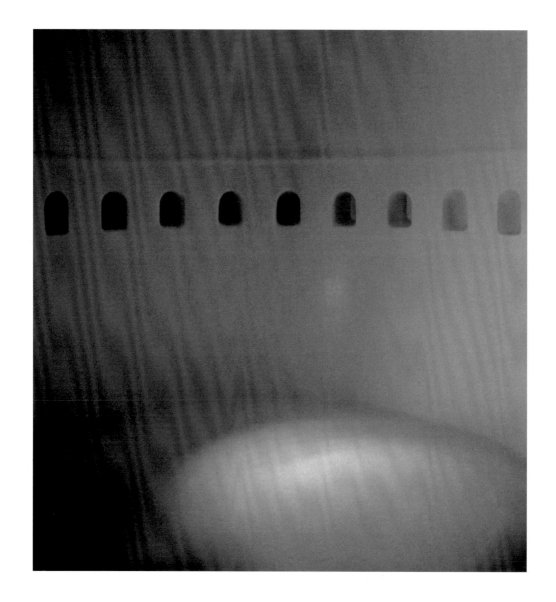

Nine Alcoves

Tall Stack of Beds *(opposite)*

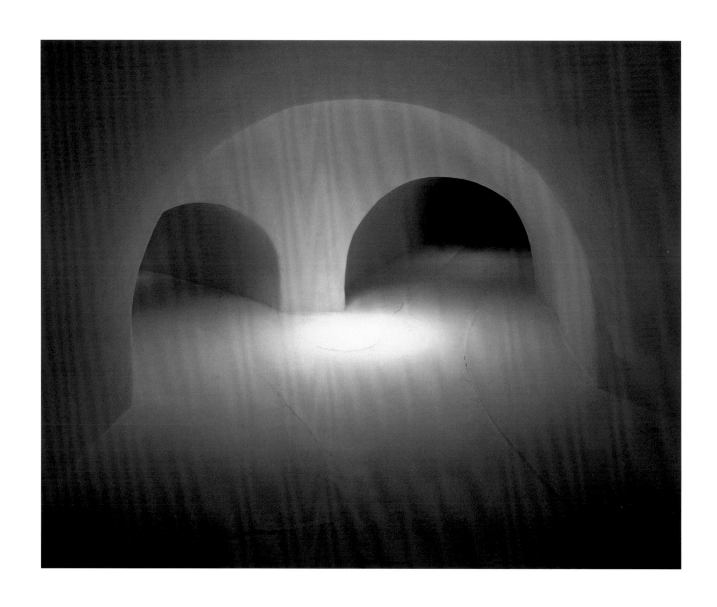

Two Tunnels from Left

Two Tunnels from Right *(opposite)*

Converging Hallways from Left

Converging Hallways from Right *(opposite)*

Andreas Gursky

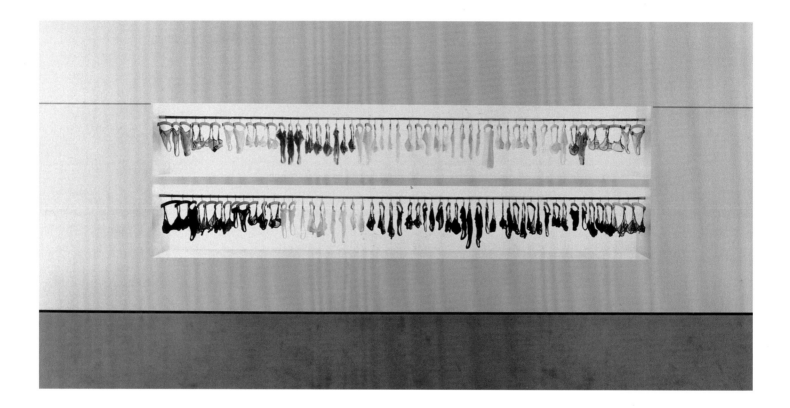

Untitled IX

Untitled IV *(opposite)*

Hong Kong, Stock Exchange (diptych)

Bundestag

San Francisco *(opposite)*

Mark Power
The Millennium Dome

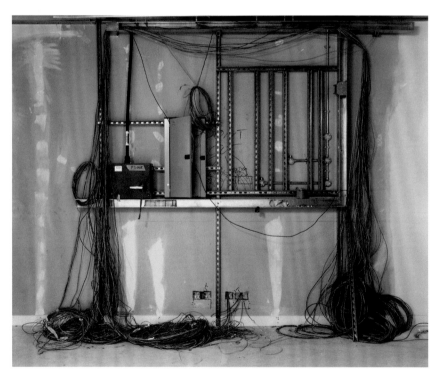

20 October 1998 *(top)* 7 October 1998 *(bottom)*

19 May 1998 *(opposite)*

1 January 1999 *(top)* 18 January 1999 *(bottom)*

9 February 1999 *(opposite)*

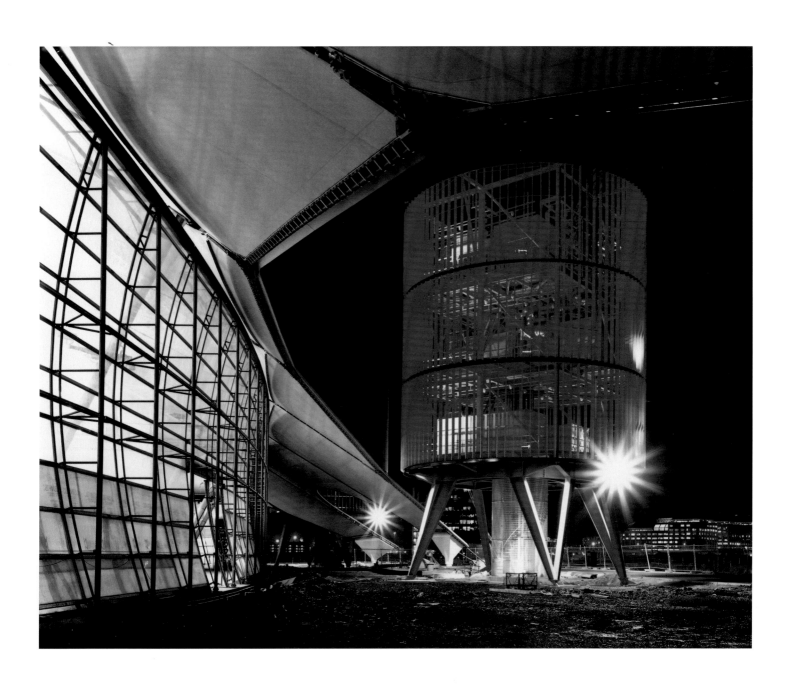

Hannah Starkey

Untitled, May 1997

Untitled, May 1997 *(opposite)*

Untitled, October 1998

Untitled, October 1998 *(opposite)*

Untitled, October 1998

Untitled, October 1998 *(opposite)*

Deborah Baker
Gaze: The Anxious Sign

Lesley Shearer
Women and Men

John Askew
Teach Yourself Russian

Толщина бумаги (The thickness of paper)

Луч звезды (The ray of the star) *(opposite left)*,   Граница поля (The border of the field) *(opposite right)*

John Stezaker

Angel

Angel (opposite)

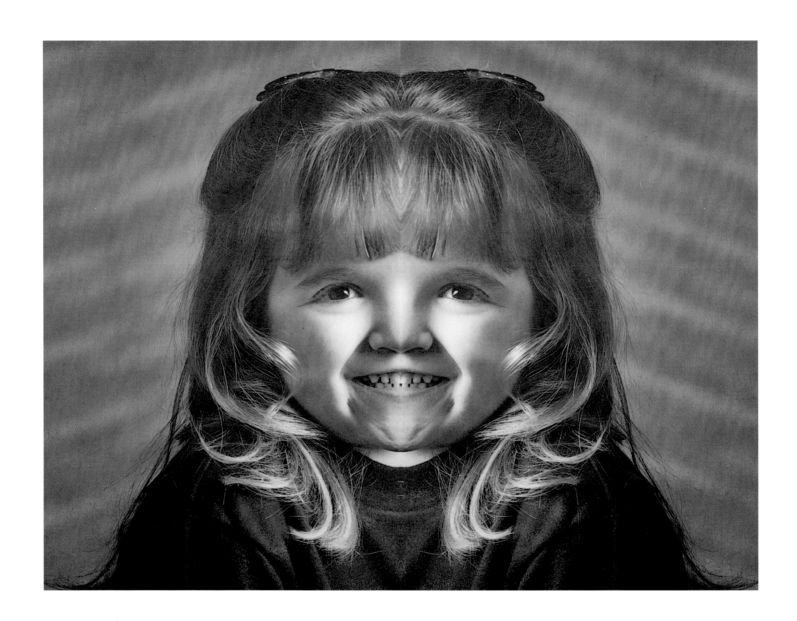

Angel

Demon *(opposite)*

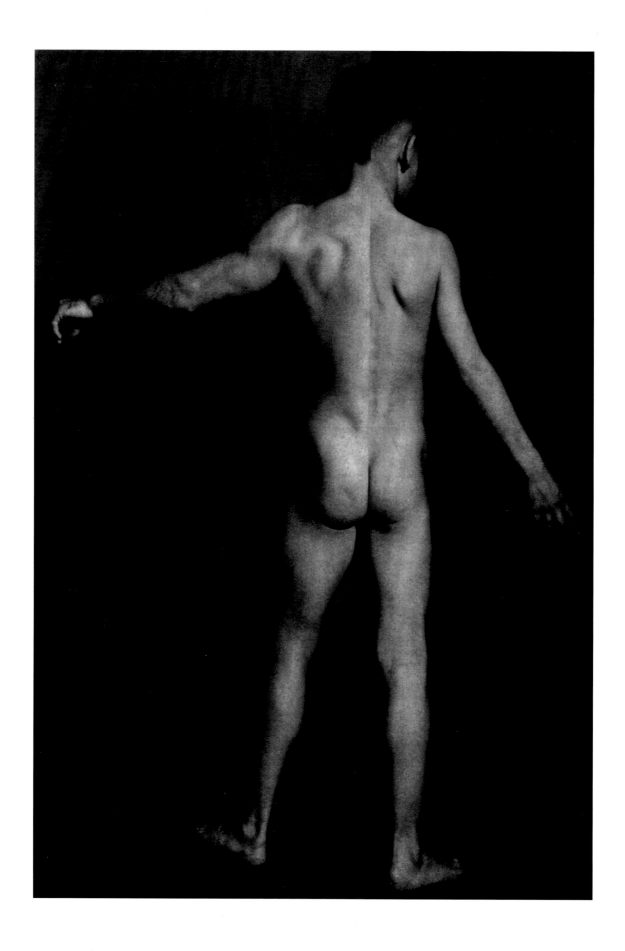

Cross

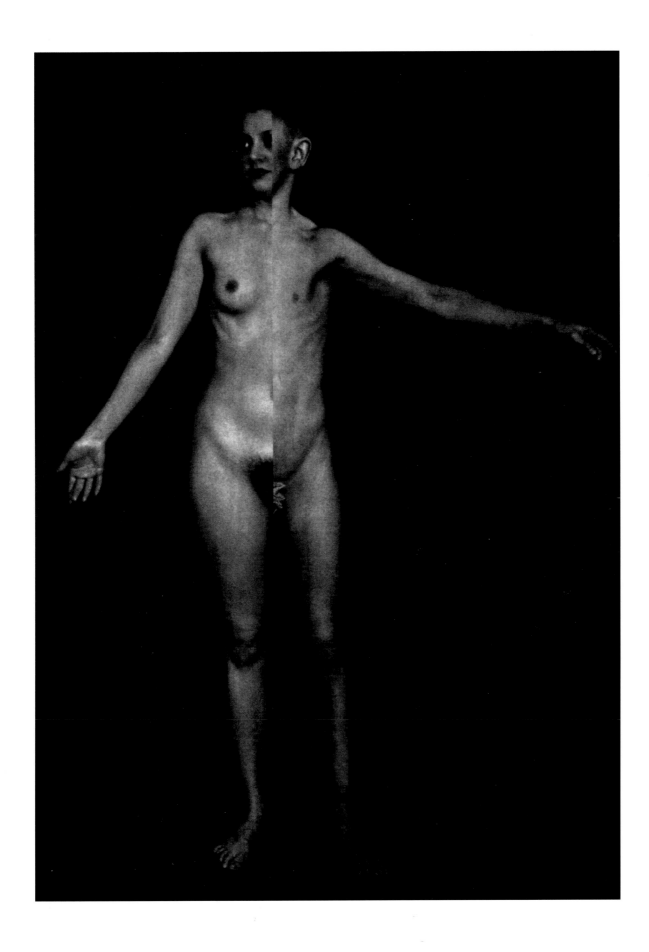

Josef Koudelka
Reconnaissance

View of Llyn Fawr, Rhigos, Heads of the Valleys

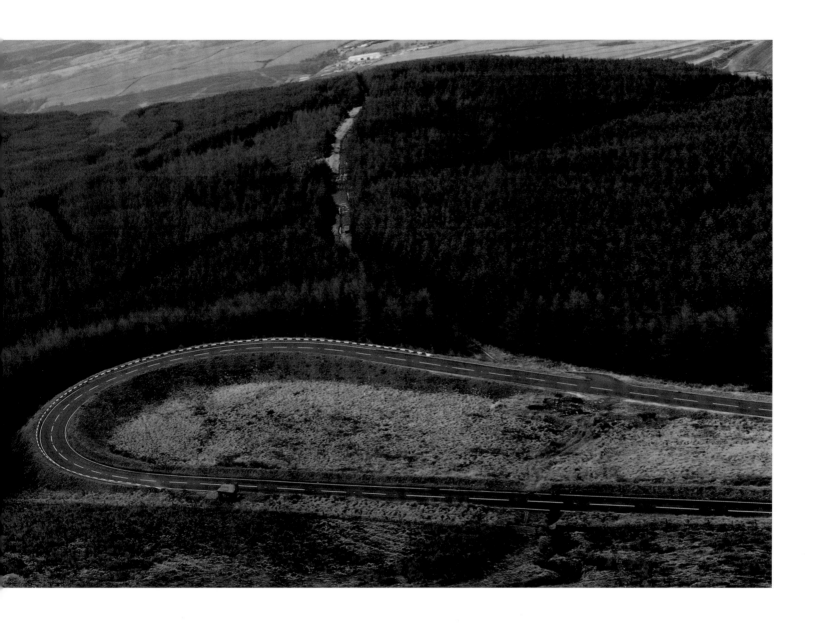

Graving Dock #1, Inner Harbour, Cardiff Bay

Jon Thompson
The Ultimate Act of Modelling

Melanie Manchot

Mrs Manchot - Bending Back

Mrs Manchot - Leaning Forward *(opposite)*

Body Study IX

Catalogue

JAMES CASEBERE
Cibachrome photographs on aluminium
Toppled Desks, 1997
61 x 76 cm
Toilets, 1995
61 x 76 cm
Two Bunk Cell, 1997
152.5 x 122 cm
Nine Alcoves, 1995
76 x 76 cm
Tall Stack of Beds, 1997
305 x 244 cm
Two Tunnels from Right, 1998
122 x 152.5 cm
Two Tunnels from Left, 1998
122 x 152.5 cm
Converging Hallways from Left, 1997
218 x 305 cm
Converging Hallways from Right, 1997
122 x 183 cm
Courtesy the Artist and Sean Kelly Gallery,
New York

ANDREAS GURSKY
Colour prints
Untitled IX, 1998
136 x 226 cm
Untitled VI, 1997
186 x 239 cm
Hong Kong Stock Exchange, 1994 (diptych)
Each work 166 x 226 cm
Bundestag, 1998
284 x 207 cm
San Francisco, 1998
267 x 197 cm
Courtesy Serpentine Gallery, London

MARK POWER
The Millennium Dome
C-type photographs
30 x 38 inches
Courtesy the Artist

HANNAH STARKEY
C-type photographs
48 x 60 inches
Courtesy the Artist and Maureen Paley,
Interim Art, London

DEBBIE BAKER
Gaze: The Anxious Sign
Video capture printed on canvas
5 x 4 feet
Courtesy the Artist

LESLEY SHEARER
Women and Men, 1998
C-type photographs
30 x 42 inches
Courtesy the Artist and Street Level
Gallery, Glasgow

JOHN ASKEW
Teach Yourself Russian, 1998
Dye transfer prints
30 x 30 inches
Courtesy the Artist

JOHN STEZAKER
Iris prints
46.5 x 61.5 inches
Courtesy the Artist

JOSEF KOUDELKA
Gelatin silver photographs, 1997-98
33 x 100 cm
Courtesy Ffotogallery, Cardiff

JON THOMPSON
Gelatin silver photograph
Untitled
150 x 240 cm
Untitled
150 x 240 cm
Courtesy the Artist

MELANIE MANCHOT
Silver Gelatin on Canvas
Mrs Manchot - Bending Back, 1996
145 x 125 cm
Mrs Manchot - Leaning Forward, 1998
134 x 110 cm
Body Study IX, 1995
150 x 145 cm
Courtesy the Artist

CONTRIBUTORS
An exhibition of **James Casebere**'s new
photographs was shown at the Museum of
Modern Art in Oxford between January and
April 1999. The tour of **Andreas Gursky**'s
retrospective exhibition includes the
Serpentine Gallery, London, and The Dean
Gallery, National Galleries of Scotland in
Edinburgh. **Mark Power** is the official
photographer for The Millennium Dome. His
photographs can be seen at the Zelda Cheatle
Gallery in London from December 1999.
Hannah Starkey's photographs were shown
at Interim Art during October and November

1998. **Deborah Baker**'s video capture images
will be shown in a forthcoming exhibition at
Midlands Art Centre, Birmingham. *Men and
Women* by **Lesley Shearer** was shown at
Street Level Gallery, Glasgow, during
December 1998. **John Askew**'s series *Teach
Yourself Russian* comprises 11 dye transfer
prints. **John Stezaker**'s exhibition *Angels* will
be shown at Portfolio Gallery during the 1999
Edinburgh International Festival in August.
Josef Koudelka's new work *Reconnaissance*
was shown at the National Museum & Gallery
of Wales, as one of four major exhibitions of
his work shown in galleries in Cardiff from
December 1998 to February 1999. **Jon
Thompson**'s forthcoming exhibition can be
seen at the Anthony Reynolds Gallery in
London. **Melanie Manchot**'s work was
shown at the Zelda Cheatle Gallery in London
during November and December 1998. A
new series of portraits of her mother will be
published as *Vile Bodies,* in late 2000.

WRITERS
David Bate is a practicing artist and is Course
Leader in MA Photographic Studies at the
University of Westminster.
David Chandler is a writer, curator and
Director of Photoworks.
Piers Masterson is a writer based in London.
David Alan Mellor is an independent
curator, writer, and Senior Lecturer in History
of Art at Sussex University.
Stella Santacatterina is a curator, writer and
freelance lecturer based in London.
Amanda Hopkinson is Senior Research
Fellow in the School of Journalism, the
University of Wales, Cardiff.
John Stathatos is an artist and writer based in
London.
Joanna Lowry is Senior Lecturer in Art
History and Media Studies at Kent Institute of
Art and Design.
Mark Durden lectures in History and Theory
of Photography at the University of Derby.
He is also an artist who, together with Paul
Rooney and David Campbell, has been
exhibiting regularly as Common Culture.
Simon Morrissey is a freelance writer and
curator based in London.
Paul Ryan is a writer and lecturer (and exile)
based in London.

ACKNOWLEDGEMENTS
John Stezaker's Iris prints are produced by
Ian Cartright of CIRCA Fine Art Digital
Printmakers, London.
Review photographs by Josef Koudelka and
Martin Parr reproduced courtesy of Magnum.

Surveillance and Solitude
James Casebere

DAVID BATE

On the wall near the entrance to James Casebere's exhibition of photographs at MOMA in Oxford is a quote from the influential French thinker Michel Foucault. It reads: "Is it surprising that prisons resemble factories, schools, barracks, hospitals, which all resemble prisons?".[1] This quote offers a way into the work and gives a sort of safety net of meanings for the spectator. Like the concept of 'discipline' in Foucault's book *Discipline and Punish,* from which this quote has been taken, the quote 'disciplines' the spectator's relation to the photographs. Discipline offers a rigour, a setting of boundaries (an essential aspect of parenthood) which at the same time acts as a constraint, a limitation. In the spirit of this ambiguity of 'discipline' the following text makes observations about Casebere's work from both within that discipline described by Foucault and without – outside of it. If Foucault's quote is taken away and the explicit reference to prisons removed, what is there left for the meaning of these pictures? What are we supposed to do with these pictures of 'empty spaces'? This 'nothing to see'? What is the point of them?

James Casebere began to receive critical attention at the beginning of the 1980s along with a group of other American artists – Cindy Sherman, Robert Longo, Sherrie Levine and Richard Prince amongst others – whom critics like Douglas Crimp first dubbed as engaged in 'The Photographic Activity of Postmodernism'. Here was a group (not actually a group, but one which could be construed) whose work drew on the legacy of what was negatively known as the 'theatricality of minimal sculpture' and the performance (body) art of the 1970s. Minimalism of course was not about a style but a way of emphasising a thing; it was emphatically a spatial art. Such interests are linked in Casebere's work.

From the pictures themselves we cannot tell the original size of the models depicted. Casebere's method is to make models, usually based on images of existing places. The models are based on two-dimensional reproductions of existing buildings. According to Casebere the actual models are not very interesting in themselves; it is when they are transformed through lighting and spaces produced through photographs that 'they come alive'. From a conventional point of view his photographs are at least three levels of remove from any actual world. These pictures of buildings are 're-interpreted' through the actual model itself and then again through the photographic process, lighting, focus, framing, depth-of-field, point-of-view and so on, which turns the models into photographs. Through this process of re-translation the artist has shaped and re-shaped these phantasmic spaces into the images that he wants, a process of simulacral construction. They become virtual places, giving up any specific reference to 'the real'. What kind of fantasy is this?

Foucault's quote is taken out of context. He does not argue that institutions such as schools, hospitals, factories and barracks are somehow *the same* as prisons; rather, that despite their differences as institutions there are similarities in their use of disciplinary power. For Foucault, power in the modern era is not something that you have and prevent others from having: it is not a punitive relation between the powerful and the powerless, that is, a power which can be exploited and abused. This is a *negative* conception of power. Foucault speaks of power relations, not social control; he argues that power is produced through types of knowledge. Knowledge *produces* power. Foucault tries to show how those knowledges have a productive effect on *all* of those acting within the institution. *Discipline and Punish* develops this thesis through a study of the modern prison where the 'orderliness' of the inmates, the prisoners, depends on a knowledge associated with looking. It is here that the 'institution' in its concrete form – as architecture – functions as a mechanism of power, enabling certain hierarchical forms of visibility, producing specific power relations 'automatically'. It is this principle of the panopticon, based on designs of the English Utilitarian social reformer Jeremy Bentham which enables a certain *régime* of vision to function as power relations. The organisation of architecture around light and lines of sight enabled a single 'super-visor' to, literally, 'oversee' a whole group of inmates – a principle followed in the designs of 19th century schools, factories, hospitals, etc. The sense of being watched which comes from this arrangement is what makes the system so generally efficient, each inmate 'internalises' this potential of 'being watched' and supposedly behaves correctly.

In James Casebere's work the spectator is offered cool points of view into 'architectural' spaces. S/he is offered a position to look within them, but not given any identity in relation to them. We are not positioned as an inmate or gaoler, but these are positions which, if we so choose, we can identify with. What the very minimal reference to the spaces does, in effect, is to foreground the spectator's own relationship to them. What position a spectator takes depends on what sort of fantasy position they have a predisposition to conceive of as viable. As always, in the geometrical viewpoint of the conventional photographic apparatus, the first position of identification for a spectator is with the camera. It is from this point-of-view that James Casebere's fantasy re-construction of actual places and spaces enables the viewer to project themselves into the spaces as they like: as omnipotent observer, as already guilty inmate, as a visitor or isolated soul. Any sense of a 'nothing to see' gives way to a sense of enmeshment with these spaces resulting in a "I don't like being 'positioned' here" or, "I don't see the point of being positioned here" or "I want to see someone" and so on, in a fantasy relation to the spaces depicted.

This is not to say that the spectator is 'imprisoned' by the pictures. Surveillance is not a uni-directional power. It is dependent on a relationship between two terms, surveyed and surveyor. Recent 'visual theory' has tended to conflate the social positions, gaoler and prisoner, the police and the citizen, the neighbourhood watch and the criminal, etc., with the psychical – psychoanalytic – concepts of voyeurism and exhibitionism. While theoretically trying to put these together might seem productive, there is nevertheless a world of difference between the prison system of surveillance and the social-psychical relations of, say, a fashion cat-walk. A panoptic prison *régime* of surveillance is based on a permanent registration of looks and gazes. It is totalitarian: private space is abolished. In so-called normal life the only permanent observation of your 'self' is by the institution of what Freud called the super-ego, that internal self-judging agency which is a composite of internalised authority figures that attempts to instil a sense of disciplinary guilt in the human subject. The emergence of surveillance systems in daily life, the electronic structures of CCTV in urban city centres, offices and private buildings, then might be seen to be competing with this as a kind of (paranoic) social super-ego. Casebere's pictures potentially trigger such feelings of judgement in relation to the spaces depicted through their sense of some 'missing' event or reason why we are 'there'.

Some commentators speak of Casebere's images as 'tableaux', but in the definition as the pictorial representation of an event, story or general moment, most of Casebere's pictures are not tableaux. They may allude to historical spaces, Greek, Victorian, Medieval, Modern, but there is no time or moment specified in the images except when an image has a temporal object within it. When an image has a cluster of tables or beds 'upturned' and stacked, or a broken toilet, what is given is a *moment* in the life of the place and the image does become a minimal tableau. Stacked beds signify the beginning or end of their use, or at least the specific depicted temporal moment of 'non-usage'. These

minimal signs (stack of beds) also signify the absence of humans, for it is the conventional function of the bed to serve human repose and activities seen as a withdrawal from the social or public sphere. Given the widespread actual closure of mental asylums in Western societies and the shift towards community care, the image might reasonably be associated with a fantasy of inmates upping and leaving institutions. But if this should seem to be the image of 'escape' it is also worth noting that Casebere in an interview describes his cell pictures as a 'celebration of solitude'.

Adam Phillips, writing about 'Risk and Solitude' remarks that "the wish for solitude can be a denial of dependence, a capacity for solitude may be its fullest acknowledgement." [2] His argument suggests that a capacity for solitude is established in infancy, for example during infantile play with the "reliable, unimpinging presence of the mother... [who] is always there presiding over our solitude". [3] If Casebere's images are phantasmic spaces in which to celebrate solitude, rather than an escape from it, then as spectators we are confronted with our 'selves' and our own body. The mother is the first of many internalised super-ego figures who can be benign rather than overbearing or oppressive. This in effect returns us to the issue of discipline and the familial network of relations in which we become 'who we are'. The sense of setting boundaries, rules, regulations, of what can and cannot be done, structure our ways of dealing with the world. Outside of Foucault, Casebere's work provokes a meditation on loneliness and solitude; relations which are, so to speak, 'contained' with a particular configuration of gazes, looks and spaces. Exactly what relation these images have to this structure of self-judgement, however, remains ambiguous and ambivalent. If these images are explorations of solitude (as incarceration) then their spatial topography might be referred to as more an 'inploration' which opens up *interiority*. Such an argument might be confirmed by the more recent pictures by Casebere, in their metaphorical allusion to the body, in monochromatic pink tunnels and tubes. Given the conventional drive of scopophilia – of pleasure in looking – to mastery, one might see Casebere's project as an attempt to master solitude (and one's body) and indeed, master the experience of incarceration. After all, to be attracted to the construction of prisons and cells as minimal ascetic spaces must show some sort of pleasure in thinking about incarceration.

TALL STACK OF BEDS, 1997

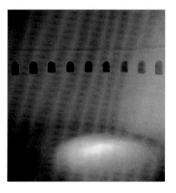

NINE ALCOVES, 1995

TWO TUNNELS FROM RIGHT, 1998

1. Michel Foucault, *Discipline and Punish* (Penguin, 1986). 2. Adam Phillips, 'On Kissing', *Tickling and Being Bored* (London: Faber & Faber, 1993) p.38. 3. Ibid.

A World Made to Order
Andreas Gursky

DAVID CHANDLER

New technology once came with the promise of a more leisurely world. New patterns of work based on increased efficiency, faster production and unlimited, instant information would reshape societies and reorder lifestyles. We would ease forward into the age of liquid information with a sigh of relief, with more time on our hands and a better quality of life. Of course, for the majority of us, what we have is more or less the reverse. More speed and efficiency has simply raised the expectations for production, now there is always more we can do. The 'instant' increasingly determines the value of (our) time; accelerating exchanges, multiple possibilities propel us forward and lift the heart rates of millions of workers across the globe. We are locked into corporate networks and structures that dictate, perhaps more than we might want to guess, the terms of our existence, what Herbert Marcuse once called our 'democratic unfreedom'.[1]

At first sight Andreas Gursky's 1994 diptych, *Hong Kong Stock Exchange*, would appear to be a graphic illustration of this state of affairs. In this work we overlook a vast hall in which row upon row of computer screens and their operators are tightly arranged. Emphatic diagonals convey the hall's volume, in sharp contrast to the restricted space allocated to each red-vested stock trader. From our elevated position the room takes on the logic of the circuit board and the numbered individuals are reduced to components in the machine. Yet social commentary is not an active agent here, as precise as Gursky's definition is we are not drawn into the picture or given the sense of an emotive human predicament. What holds the artist's fascination and our attention in this work is its formal rigour; the overwhelming yet monotonous detail that trails off into the distance; the colour transitions that lighten as they rise through the deep red carpet and the traders' vests to wall screens and ceiling; and the grid-like connections that tie everything together. In addition, by setting the two pictures together, Gursky reinvents the hall, skewing it into an illusory V-shape and making something almost expressionistic from its formal potential. The work is happily artificial and, with its undertow of realism, it produces a heightened sense of the place itself as a construction, of a world made to order.

The *Hong Kong Stock Exchange* is a useful introduction to the growing preoccupations of Gursky's more recent work as he moves towards a more formal approach. Since the early 1980s he has shown us scenes composed of patterns and structures that echo from one place to another

in what has become a global project. These structures confer an order within which human life is increasingly prescribed; people are routinely compliant, they wander through tightly controlled and demarcated public spaces, they are marshalled into groups or stand dazed in the face of maps or strange topographies for which they have temporarily lost the key. Repetition and a sense of the unbounded infinite inform this condition. Gursky's pictures often encompass large distances and a visible strata of information from which we imagine a world of complex interconnections and interrelated micro- and macro-structures. Here the search for the sublime in nature – that in their epic scale and sweeping vistas Gursky's works make reference to – is ironically repositioned in culture (or in what Gursky has called an 'aggregate state') where it often discovers beauty in the banal. The world is organised and controlled along formal lines that mirror the developing language of art. Gursky works with that point of transformation where one is appropriated by the other.

In the *Hong Kong Stock Exchange* pictures human movement is subdued, but it is the slight variations in the traders' behaviour, their confined, fidgeting gestures that holds most of our detailed attention. In other such spaces, for example on trader floors in Tokyo, Chicago and Singapore, the collective human display is more vigorous, and in this sense these pictures join with those of raves to form an interesting, parallel strand in Gursky's progress towards greater abstraction. In both sets of pictures the artist frames theatres of unrestrained physical action and interaction, but in each case the chaotic group is either spatially contained or unified by a governing language, or both. Just as the digital display boards provide the number code and controlling system to the traders' exaggerated, dandyish flourishes, so the DJ in *Union Rave* (1995) signals the pace and rhythm of the dance. Similarly the great circular lighting tracks that hover above the revellers in *May Day* (1997) are a form of diagrammatic representation of each dancer's somatic space, through which, like the red circles above, they intersect and overlap. The culturally disparate physical freedoms of financial exchange and hedonism here submit to a governing order, just as graphic elements they are unified by the photograph.

In his gradual shift towards the reconstruction and abstraction of visual information (through the use of digital technology), Gursky has also revealed more explicity his interest in painting and pictorial traditions. In works such as the photographs of skies, *Untitled II* (1993) and *Untitled VII*

(1998) and the image of a shadowed gravel surface *Untitled III* (1996), for example, he has flirted with the idea of the 'formless' in art[2], something given a further twist in two photographs that show paintings by J.M.W. Turner and Jackson Pollock, *Turner Collection* (1995) and *Untitled VI* (1997). In 1816 William Hazlitt offered an astute appraisal (and for him a critique) of Turner's developing style that might serve the work of Gursky just as well: "[Turner's] ...pictures are too much abstractions of aerial perspective, and representations not properly of the objects of nature as of the medium through which they are seen. They are the triumph of the knowledge of the artist... over the barrenness of the subject...."[3] Gursky's image of three Turner paintings is instructive in that the painter represents a moment of fracture between the subject and the autonomy of the work of art. Turner's creation of an amorphous abstraction, his dissolution of form into areas of pure colour (that significantly coincided with the appearance of photography[4]), was singular and transgressive, a wilful breaking with an ordered tradition, an 'expressive' moment driven by a fiercely independent ambition. Similar things might be said of Pollock's achievement at another point along the course of modern painting, and to see these artists' work here in the minimal, mute, and ear-splittingly loud, blankness of the modern gallery space provides the dry tension on which Gursky's art habitually feeds. These pictures again explore the imposition of order, the replotting of individual, unprogrammed action into more rigid cultural systems, but, perhaps more than this, they consider the distancing effect of the doubled process of presentation and representation that Gursky's works complete.

The convergent spaces of museums and shops provide a natural context for Gursky's more recent concerns. Their shared modes of display are a kind of abstraction in themselves, a shorthand that accounts for the 'aura' of the object within the language of contemporary consumer culture. The point of sale and the point of encounter have merged; all relevant information, history, knowledge is now encoded in the product/exhibit and the display is refined into a kind of minimal spell of desire and attraction. Logically this 'condensing' or stripping away could evaporate the goods altogether as in Gursky's photograph *Prada II* (1997), but the intensity of the experience remains unaltered: here the retail space becomes a state of mind.

One of Gursky's most prominent 'shop' pictures is the digitally constructed *Untitled V* (1997), showing over

two hundred trainers uniformly displayed on back-lit white shelving. Gursky's throwaway explanation of this work as a comment on 'the fetishism of our material world' does not account for its particular resonance or its connection with his work in general. Although the image takes its cue from real sports shoe displays, in Gursky's obsessive rearrangement the trainers have become artworks, or perhaps an artwork. Each shoe is a microcosm of abstracted signs where line and colour strain form and function. Their designs employ a kind of cartoon language of swirls, morphed stripes, distortion and layering that derives from graffiti and the heavily ritualised anarchies of the street. In this airless, lifeless space they are stand-ins for human movement and physical expression. Given the currency of graffiti, automatism and the so called 'primitive' that provided the base aesthetic for Pollock's action painting to emerge, Gursky's *Untitled V* and *VI* have a strange but insistent affiliation.

Like all Gursky's works the scale of *Untitled V* threatens to overwhelm the viewer. It also carries something common to much of his work: the idea of 'excess', that can be (and knowingly so on the part of the artist) both enthralling and dispiriting. This sense in Gursky's work is brought to its most visually taxing pitch in the recent architectural abstractions, in those works, for example, based on hotel spaces in *Atlanta* (1996) and *Times Square* (1997). These pictures, together with *Ayamonte* (1997) are Gursky's most extreme in the sense of the viewer's displacement. They chart the falling away of representation into pattern and form, held at a point where residual elements of photographic record fade into the hybrid image, a digital abstraction, neither photograph or painting. The endlessly repeated grids and decorative motifs in these works and the sense of flatness pulling against a contorted spatial depth, serves to enhance the feeling of an 'excess' of production tied to a bare economy of human experience. As the architectural units are multiplied and space is swept beyond perceptual logic there is a sense of fatigue in the image, and a trace of hysteria too. The gentle gridded harmonies of *Paris, Montparnasse* (1993) are here replaced by a mind-numbing loop of elevator jingles played at deafening volume.

1. Herbert Marcuse, *One Dimensional Man*, 1964.
2. For a discussion around the idea of the 'formless' in art see *Formless: A User's Guide*, Yve-Alain Bois and Rosalind Kraus, 1997.
3. Quoted in Lawrence Gowring, *Turner: Imagination and Reality*, Museum of Modern Art, New York, 1966, p13.
4. Turner's interest in photography in the years before his death in 1851 is well documented. See James Hamilton, *Turner: A Life*, 1997, or Mary Warner Marien, *Photography and its Critics: A Cultural History 1839-1900*, 1997.

UNTITLED VI, 1997

PRADA II, 1997

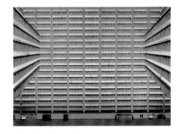

TIMES SQUARE, 1997

The Millennium Dome
Mark Power

DAVID CHANDLER

Staked out by a bend in the river the unfinished Millennium Dome is strangely submerged compared to the rising, aspirational domes of architectural history. With its stretched white canopy and massive pylons it brings to mind a circus top or an empty gas cylinder. It has the look of something already spent. But perhaps its closest relation is that fun-phantom of post-war popular culture, the flying saucer. The Dome aspires to the longed-for thrill of a UFO landed in our midst, which, in the collective imagination (courtesy of Speilberg), we enter to find a technological dream-world that is also a 21st century spiritual heaven. Satisfying dreams is a tricky business, especially when matched against the cost of basic human needs, but, for better or for worse, this is what the Millennium Dome has set out to do.

Given fresh impetus by the arrival of the new government in 1997, the building of the Dome has become an important test site for New Labour's modern vision. Here, finally, is something on a grand physical scale, against which their central idea of 'the modern' might be easily calibrated by a mass audience. As such the Dome's function has come to signify a break with the past and another gesture of dismissal for the Tory's continual reliance on the past to underpin and justify the ideological present. And yet the Dome is a temporary structure for which the civic ambitions are bluntly short-term. It will not survive as a landmark, it will not even become a piece of Nineties nostalgia. Instead the short-life Dome seems already defined as an expensive passing show.

As if to provide something lasting, to insert the weight of history against this transitory image, Mark Power has been commissioned to record the building of the Dome from bare patch of wasteland to completion. Given its public sensitivity, the task of 'interpreting' this brief is a uniquely difficult one. However, his work on the site to date manages to transcend expectations, accommodating both the physical resonance of the growing building and its status as an event imbued with political and social tension. What his photographs suggest is that through all the speculations, criticisms and the emerging images of its final form, the real sense of achievement and enterprise that the Dome represents – its dignity – may well lie in the spectacular process of its construction. This is what Power has set out to record and this is what he interprets as a haunting blend of grandeur and fantasy.

The idea that the construction of a building might warrant and benefit from photographic attention came as part of photography's expansion into all areas of society in the mid-19th century. While not as fleeting as a wave breaking on a shore or the orderly chaos of a city street, recording the growth of a building – seeing architecture as a process, one of significant moments that could be reconstructed into a narrative – found a logic through photography. The two disciplines both expressed altered patterns of time and space: just as the new building materials and methods spawned by industrialisation created grids of iron frame and reinforced concrete, carving up space into new geometries with new perspectives, so photography segmented and re-ordered time. The images from the early negotiations between architecture and photography still retain the vigour and immediacy of a new aesthetic in embryo, of new fields of perception being opened up. Such memorable encounters, from Phillip Henry Delamotte's album of 1855 that records the rebuilding of the Crystal Palace, to Durandelle and Chevojon's photographs of the construction of the Eiffel Tower (1888) and Delmaet and Durandelle's epic documentary on the building of the Paris Opera (1861-75), lay the foundation for modernist photography of 40 years later.

What these pioneering series achieve, and what is interesting for Power looking back at them, is that they literally 'monumentalise' the process of construction. In each photograph the building assumes a distinct identity; structures change, spatial relationships and volumes are redefined and light is redirected. What the images come to represent is a series of different buildings, or a series of 'monuments' to the final building. As if to counter the image of the ruin in picturesque art, that might denote a reverence for things past and suggest time slipping slowly back to an idyllic moment that might be regained, images of construction sites and skeletal buildings created monuments to time pressing forward; they looked to the future and spoke of an accelerated sense of change. Charged with the inevitability of progress, they celebrated the dynamic imperative of society's unfinished business.

It would be difficult to sustain meaningful links between this sense of purpose, of modernity in the making, and the building of the Millennium Dome – with its hollow PR and deeply ironic civic status – in the late 20th century. But what Mark Power does here is to take the idea of a building driven by a kind of 'social energy', with all the crisp language of a 'new vision' that the 19th century had to offer, and work something of a 'de-construction' on it. What is it, he seems to ask in this work, to create a building that reflects and embraces a new millennium in an era of liberated signs and meanings, of fractured, reflected images and simulations, when a building might be anything other than just a building.

In a way this multi-faceted, prising open of the building process became a product of Power's investigation of the site as it changed. As his first commission of this kind, his approach has evolved as a form of discovery, through many days spent searching, poking around, assessing angles and distances, light levels and patterns, interpreting the language of the site as it offered, revealed and reconstituted itself. Amid all the practical problems and frustrations of working on the site with a large-format camera, Power's work has developed into a project with several interlocking lines of enquiry.

In the first instance, and largely through the black-and-white imagery of the social war zone, he considered the transmutation of the site from toxic dump to a place fit for work and the triumphal symbolism of millennial celebration. This first phase of the building was an immense exercise in itself, with its own battlefield landscape of mud pools, twisted iron, earth-wounds and scars. Under grim winter daylight, and the occasional glistening nocturne of arc-lights, showing off the pin-pricked silhouette of Canary Wharf (a kind of parental presence overlooking the building of the Dome and a constant marker in Power's work), the unholy ground is churned and flattened out. Through this Power's photographs carry signs of human submersion; jokey of course, but, like the image of a group of bloodied, severed gloves scattered around a sacrificial block, they are full of an unspecified but insistent sense of human cost.

Emerging from what could be taken as the site of some catastrophe, a thing reported on, a place of clues and evidence, Power begins to celebrate the fabulous mechanics of the building, an orchestration of human endeavour that gradually changes pitch as the elements of a giant three-dimensional jigsaw are locked into place. By any measure this was and is an epic event, one that demands distance and a calculated response. But in the face of its sheer scale, the overwhelming, almost cartoon size of the architectural components, in whose presence one has a tingle of nervous excitement, Power's work has not fallen sterile or become overly analytical. He delights in the soaring pylons, in the delicate tracery of wires and steel cables, and on the site floor he is distracted by the brute form and endless

repetition of building materials and equipment. The entire theatrical process of such a huge space being systematically delineated and contained is met, in Power's work, by photographs that blend wide-eyed wonder with the precision and discipline of architects' drawings. In his sectioned images, full of bold, exquisite symmetries, fine lines and overlapping squares and circles, it is as though Power's camera had become part of the building, integrated into the architectural performance.

As the building edges nearer towards its final form and the interior space becomes more cluttered, so the distanced view with its epic proportions has become more difficult to establish and less representative of the site. In Power's most recent work in the Dome we are led into smaller spaces, half-built rooms and soon-to-be public areas primed with another atmosphere and a different aesthetic. If scale and space dictated the terms of the earlier work, now colour dominates the vocabulary: from pale cellophane washes to primary acid glare. In these 'interiors' colour now defines space and a certain tension too. Power often pictures these rooms as carefully laid traps, glowing with a sinister yet alluring energy and light. Here strange configurations of objects, lights, equipment and building site detritus have their own alien logic, electricity seems dangerously exposed, not yet diverted through walls and ducts. As the Dome prepares to process its audience, these wild, techno-spaces suggest a building charging-up, coming to life, yet one that is wilfully inhospitable. This is the pre-calmed, pre-textured Dome, raw and undecorated, exotic and dangerous, unfit for human use.

Impressions of the finished Dome suggest it will fall somewhere between a fun-palace (yes, there will be a circus!) and a kind of gaudy prison. The thought occurs: will we be forced to go? Perhaps, like Blade Runner, it will be as much mediaeval market as transcendent futuristic trip. But now, under Power's gaze, as some great flying ship emerging from a high-tech mud swamp, the Dome holds on to its structural beauty, and expresses a release of human energy and ingenuity moving forward at a relentless pace. If the end result is unremittingly bright, a grievous assault on the senses, then Mark Power's Dome is a place of subtle light and colour transitions that, without the irritant of building noise, has a gentle, spectral silence. This dense network of chambers, wire grids, steel, plate glass and factory fresh materials is indeed a site to marvel at. Here construction itself is the millennial spectacle, the condition of a magical space.

2 FEBRUARY 1998

19 MAY 1998

21 JANUARY 1998

Anatomy of Boredom
Hannah Starkey

PIERS MASTERSON

I'm bored, the Chairman of the Bored - Iggy Pop

It is a Saturday night. You have worked your way through the meagre list of phone numbers in your address book (is it really true that after nearly 30 years on this planet your entire social network can fit on to one sheet of A5)? You leave the same message on a succession of answerphones. "Hi it's XXXXX. Haven't seen you for some time. Thought it would be good to meet up. Give us a call, or I'll try to catch you later." Other people have social lives, having dinner parties or hanging out in those cool bar/club/restaurants described in the trendy magazines. All you have to keep you company is a bottle of Vodka and, if you're lucky, cable TV.

The imagery of boredom surrounds us; just look at the current batch of TV advertisements. Eighties ads were all hyper-kinetic designer guys and girls in their designer flats. Venetian blinds and Audi cars abounded and everything looked like a Ridley Scott movie. Nineties ads feature bored looking mothers and teenagers sullenly contemplating life with washing tablets and stay-pressed shirts. Everything looks like a Mike Leigh film. Nineties pop culture was always destined to be retro from the outset, but in its bored torpor has chosen to take as its principal source the Seventies, a decade which already had retro to spare. We will slide out of the century to a soundtrack of Fleetwood Mac and Abba cover versions.

There is a distinction to be made between what I mean by this current bored attitude and the concept of banality often discussed in postmodernism. Banality can be used to categorise a number of vernaculars, but broadly describes certain value systems of high capitalism that were to be derided or reacted to; for example, the banality of suburban living. Postmodern banality achieved a position of Zen-like contemplation, as found in the music of Laurie Anderson and David Byrne; in David Lynch's series 'Twin Peaks', or in the artworks of Sherrie Levine and Jeff Koons. This does imply a critical attitude: we can recognise the banal because it is remote from us. In the instance of the cited artists, banality is kept at arm's length by being framed with irony. Banality also legitimised the continued production and consumption of commodities, while boredom presents a state of consumer apathy. It is the nature of boredom that it is a cycle. The condition of being bored, similar to depression, is such that by the time you recognise that it exists you are already in it. With its 'om' nature, the bored culture has a totalitarian quality to it, a sense of oppression if you will. There is no alternative.

The photography of Hannah Starkey is particularly well located to capture this experience of boredom. As a practitioner she straddles fine art photography, editorial fashion shoots (most recently in the pages of Vogue) and advertising commissions. The last of these has had a significant contribution to the bored aesthetic, as already mentioned. Fashion photography is boring by its very nature and, in looking at Hannah Starkey's work, we should make a separation between the concerns of 'art' and 'fashion'. Despite the claims of some recent exhibitions, fashion cannot influence art, since by its very nature it is a derivative medium.[1] The representations of the fashion world do filter into art as part of the reflection of popular culture. Any contemporary concern with an art/fashion synthesis is just another wave of Seventies nostalgia for the never-never-land of Andy Warhol, enthroned at Studio 54, as photographed by Billy Name. Discussion of that sphere of representations properly belongs within the arena of the banal as we may understand it in its more conventional usage. It is precisely because Hannah Starkey has on a regular basis to work through the self-conscious crassness of lifestyle magazines that, when it comes to her exhibition work, she is able to openly depict the scenarios of boredom.

The temporal experience of boredom is a closed loop, outside of life's normal continuum. In the titles of her recent series the scenes are described either by physical location or by the month of the photograph; they are dislocated in time and space. The environs Hannah Starkey portrays are divested of a time frame. They are a sharp contrast with Cindy Sherman's film stills series, where the implication of the single image being a moment of a dramatic sequence was a strong part of the dynamic of the work. Hannah Starkey's photographs imply a protracted time moment. The two women sitting in the bar look as if they have been there all day, and will remain there for some time. The daylight that enters from behind the young woman's head is watery and grey, one of those overcast days when the light does not change from dawn to dusk and the listlessness is high. The figures in Hannah Starkey's photographs appear to be living impoverished lives. This is not just a reflection of their financial situation, although they may be victims of our permanently low-growth economy. While many contemporary photographers choose to focus still on a superficial profundity of experience, what makes

Hannah Starkey's work so interesting is its concentration on a type of washed out/washed up lifestyle.

Looking at Hannah Starkey's photographs you wonder why we bother to go on living. She proposes cases for 'mercy killing' as the lives she portrays have become terminally ill with boredom. They are people holding on to the pretence of aesthetic experience or social engagement, living an artificially extended existence that has lost its dignity. A repeated pose found in Hannah Starkey's scenes is the figure with its head resting on its propped hand. This is the ultimate body language of boredom as it immobilises the head, making it clear that you are indifferent to your surroundings and, if the jaw rests on the hand, it increases the effort of speaking. So the figures in Hannah Starkey's photographs are intellectually inactive, their state of boredom manifesting itself as an abdication from the sphere of communication. The limp necks, along with the inexpressive faces of these figures, underlines the sense that mental atrophy has set in.

The absence of signs of any inner life results in the concentration of the viewer on the incidental details in order to construct personas for Hannah Starkey's models. Inevitably given the photographer's other working engagements, fashion issues play a part in this. Two young women are shown wearing identical outfits; we are left to wonder if this is a cheesy corporate uniform or if, by coincidences of class, earnings, reading the same magazines, or shopping at the same store, the duplication had arisen. Perhaps because of her proximity to the fashion industry, Hannah Starkey shows clothing becoming both uniform and emblematic. The young woman wearing her Arsenal team shirt may be displaying her membership of the tribe: then again she may never have seen a football match in her life and could have adopted the shirt as a purposefully inappropriate costume. In another work we see a woman seriously contemplating herself in a changing-room mirror, knowing full well that the new garment is basically identical to dozens of others in the shop.

That picture of the Arsenal-shirt-wearing-woman keeps coming back to me as a potent image for the atomisation of subcultures that has been a feature of the last decade. Hannah Starkey's striking earlier photographs of two girls sitting post-club surrounded by cigarette ends and empty beer glasses has a similar effect. Their 'bombed' attitude has some similarity to Reneke Djikstra's video portraits of ravers in mid-trip, but in Hannah Starkey's

scenario the youths are well 'out' of it rather than 'in' to it. The clubbing scene has been so completely assimilated by the mainstream that the two bored teens look thoroughly disenchanted by the sanctioned space of their youthful rebellion. In this country the boundaries of class and employment have been eroded by the realisation that a significant number of those who consider themselves to be working-class are the long-term unemployed from middle-class backgrounds. In the early Nineties, cultural commentators in North America made great play of the emergence of Generation X, the children of the Seventies who, regardless of class backgrounds, were never going to be as economically productive as their parents. From looking at Hannah Starkey's work we can chart the emergence of a generation who are not only earning less than their parents but are having less of a good time.

If the measure of a good work of art is whether it reveals a truth, then Hannah Starkey's work is good. Her work exposes a general failure of humanity, while at the same time recognising that coping with failure is a core experience of the human condition. Hannah Starkey's photography also draws attention to the artificiality of the medium in which she works; the settings are just a bit too set-like, the models' attitudes just a bit too posed. The lure of fashion is its claim to generate fantasy. Hannah Starkey's anti-fashion imagery uses the same techniques and manipulations to generate reality.

1. I am thinking here of the exhibitions 'Addressing the Century' at the Hayward Gallery and 'Sightings' at the Institute of Contemporary Art

UNTITLED – OCTOBER 1998

UNTITLED – OCTOBER 1998

Fearful Symmetry
John Stezaker

DAVID ALAN MELLOR

These optically disturbed and disturbing portraits of children, sourced from a defunct London modelling agency directory for 1993, were originally the sites of parents' investment in their offspring's image. The *Angels* transform the institution of the groomed 'little angel', which in the USA has thrown up the posthumous fascination with Jon-Benet Ramsey, the star of children's beauty pageants. For more than 20 years John Stezaker has turned to that troubled topic of representing babies, infants and children within contemporary cultural frameworks of meaning. In 1985 the ball-headed babies in his *Egg Burial* bore the features of Tyra Banks, an infant whose death at her parents' hands was one of the catalytic instances for placing on the national agenda the issue of child abuse in the 1980's, anamorphically wrapping the portrait of Tyra over spherical surfaces. It is this fantastic use of visual geometries and perspectives which arises again in the *Angels* series. They depend upon the crossing of rays – that inversion of zones and bodily surfaces which provide the support for the *Cross Pieces,* works which have also preoccupied Stezaker during the last decade. The *Angels* are produced by unfeasible conjunctions and splicings: they turn upon the specular, the mirroring of one half of a child's full face to duplicate it into faces of perfection, triumphs of absolute and exact reflection. They possess a 'fearful symmetry', a trimming as part of the grooming – enacted now by Stezaker rather than proud parent – which then generates some closure of the visual system, some frightening conclusion by which bi-laterality, as a form of being in the world, is clamped shut over difference and the erratics of the body. The *Cross Pieces,* meanwhile, open up difference in such a way that male and female bodies are intermixed, trafficking in the impossible merging of sexual difference, while exhibiting the scar at the edge of gender's divide. The divide of sexual difference is also the primary structuring device for the *Angels*: there is only one boy, *Demon,* as opposed to the almost universal female angels. They are all sinister, but is the left side the original side of the face? Stezaker's *Angels* rhetorically resemble visual palindromes, a lateral traversing of the face where the viewer searches for the passing of the scar or split around which the face is organised, waiting until the return of the known physiognomic terrain from which they have just departed. It is this foreclosed certainty – that there can be no other aspect to the face than that which lies to one side – that entails an absence of any kind of difference, the impossibility of any otherness and which lends a peculiar structure of

dread to these *Angels*.

Their gaze is one of the most compelling elements in the series' ensemble of effects. It is a familiar gaze, in one sense, the gaze of the baleful, knowing and powerful alien children in John Wyndham's novel, *The Midwich Cuckoos*. In another inversion of meaning, the *Angels* resemble not innocents but Gorgons with lethal stares. Like Perseus we see them by a ruse with a mirror, trying to nullify their deadly gaze. Like 7th century BC depictions of the Gorgon, the Angels appear bi-corporate, *en face*, almost two creatures with one head.[1] Splay-eyed, with vast parallax – they are focused upon us. What we, as spectators, look into and find in the *Angels* is their un-negotiable gaze and it may be that a Lacanian definition of the gaze might be helpful in understanding the unsettling effects of Stezaker's series. "The gaze marks the point in the object (in the picture) from which the subject viewing it is already gazed at... the horror of coming face to face with my double is that this encounter reduces me to the object-gaze. In other words, the part missing in the mirror-image of myself... is my own gaze...."[2] In such a way the viewer of Stezaker's *Angels* is regarded and Stezaker's own gaze, his evaluation of the mirror's image, is present too, as another trace of vision, in his bifurcated construction of the child's stare.

Stezaker's intention was that his formal strategy of cutting and duplication would "chase redundancy"[3], through the stereotyped and idealised serial portrait photographs and flush out another level of significance, precipitating a "weird aberrancy"[4]. These aberrations are firstly formal or rather perspectival: aberrations in the sense and title of Jurgen Baltrusaitis' book on anamorphic projections, *Aberrations,* one rooted in the geometries of optics and representation. It is this level of uncanniness of vision – the cuttings, reflections, graftings which mark his recent body of work. The only flaw in this symmetry and what has to be erased from the final, exhibited Iris print in the *Angels*, is the vertical cut, the central divide and splice of the collage of xerox scans. This spatial division cuts but also sutures together the 'good side' of the children. The axis is the crucial point for the *Cross Piece* set, as well. But in all cases the cut itself, the seam, has disappeared and in the *Angels* this suppression is virtual, through electronic printing. But this very seamlessness provokes uncomfortable feelings for the viewer. Division becomes a binding thing and the *Angels* are confined in their own infolding, so that they cannot – yet – become sovereign subjects. And as children they are, as well, bounded by a certain fantasy of perfection: a narcissistic form of self-regard in the turning of the half-face towards itself is registered, in addition to the doubling, by reflection, upon an already believed ideal of childhood which the parents, inveigled into the children's modelling scheme, already possessed, one which is drastically revealed by Stezaker's interruption and disturbance of the photo-portraits.

The *Angels* are close cousins to a certain depicted population in children's fiction, the more than human scaled-down children, who comprise those luring denizens of Christina Rossetti's *Goblin Market* for instance. Such visual dexterity in ludic and grotesque mirroring as Stezaker has used, and an artist such as Rex Whistler utilised before him[5] comes hedged around with cautions and apprehensions about its magic. The confection of Jon-Benet Ramsey is associated with a lethal outcome and the *Angels*, like Rossetti's goblins, are sources of dangerous wonder. The child's doll or puppet has stood as a marker of the uncanny in modernist culture,[6] an invincible, untiring double of the insufficient human body. The dummy's head and the uncanny child find a point of reference for Stezaker from his reservoir of favoured film images; particularly Michael Redgrave's ventriloquist's doll in *At Dead of Night* (1945) – the prototype malign child-dummy of the kind which haunted the film referent in the Jamie Bulger case – Chuckie, from *Child's Play*. Their faces seem squashed, like talking heads on wide-screen TV sets and their identities stretched by repetition into oppressive visages: mendacious meanings spring, or are implicit in these mirrored doll-like images. Stezaker mistrusts but is fascinated by the ornamented, fetishised portrait, the child as idol, the majestic infant doubled in *Baby Colossus* which seems, in its duplicated state, to be an embodiment of something surplus, that in-human extra.[7]

Stezaker's utilisation of the mirror image may have had one of its initial points of origin in his 1970's reading of the 17th century gnostic philosopher Jakob Boehme's *De Signatura Rerum*. Here he discovered a theory of the Fall that was contingent on the passing on and weakening of the vital divine spark in humankind through "ever more remote worlds of reflective self-enclosure and self-delusion"[8]. In the mid-1970s Stezaker used Boehme's idealism of a falling away from some originary unitary divinity also as a means of 're-focusing' Marxist critiques of the commodity such as Guy Debord's *Societe du Spectacle*: "The commodity image on reflection seemed in Boehme's terms to create a mirror-hall

of infinite reduplications"[9]. In 1974-75 he produced *The Reflections Series*. In *Mould and Cast*, from that series, he used texts from Nietzsche and Marx on self-deluding ideological fantasms: "Before a hundred mirrors/before yourself false... strangled in your own net/Self knower/Self executioner/."[10] *Mould and Cast* displayed two sides of a frontal female portrait vertically stretched, a split mirror image, her face pointed, as if in a fairy-tale, like one of Richard Dadd's elves or a malign nymph. The danger of intoxication and enslavement to a specular image, as thematised by Stezaker, was also early indicated in his *Reflections* series in 1975, with photographs of a woman in thrall to the camera lens and patriarchy, mirrored vertically, doubled and with the words CAPTIVITY and CAPTURE superimposed. Thus the Fall from some originary essence is located at the moment of specular representation which produces some bounded, gross surplus. If Stezaker's *Angels* are distinctly otherworldly, they exist as countervailing images, transvaluations that mimic specular debasement, but also making strange the business enterprise and familial fantasy that first circulated these portraits of children. These *Angels* are disruptive manifestations, interruptions which transform the quotidian. This view is based by Stezaker on notions of the angelic which are found in James Hillman's 1983 essay, *Imaginal Practice: Greeting the Angel*[11], where the contemporary world encounters a weird intervention from the numinous. Such angels, in Hillman's view, become *psychopompos*, guides for the imagination that will re-orient the beholder from the fallen world of commodities: as Stezaker has projected it, a monstrous child has taken on this apocalyptic role, pristine and awesome.

ANGEL

DEMON

CROSS

1. Cf. D. Napier, *Masks, Transformations and Paradox*, University of California Press, London, 1986 p.105.
2. S. Zizek, *Looking Awry*, MIT Press, Cambridge, 1992, p.125.
3. John Stezaker, in discussion with the author, 31 March 1999.
4. Ibid.
5. Compare Stezaker's symmetries with Rex Whistler's *!OHO!* series of equivalent, reversible and upside down portrait heads, which he titled with a palindrome, cf. Rex and Laurence Whistler *!OHO!*, Lane, Harmondsworth, 1946; also L. Whistler, *Rex Whistler*, Art and Technics, London 1958, p.62.
6. Cf. R.E. Hubert, *Surrealism and the Book*, California University Press, Berkeley, 1988 pp. 150-1.
7. Cf. D. Simpson, *Fetishism and Imagination* John Hopkins University Press, London, 1982, pp.20-30. For David Simpson there is then a short step from the image of multiplied surplus to one of commodities. This linkage was at the heart of some of Stezaker's own conceptual photo-pieces in the mid-1970's.
8. John Stezaker, Letter to the author, 9th April 1999.
9. Ibid.
10. Cf. *John Stezaker*, Kunstmuseum Luzern 1979, pp. 8-9.
11. J. Hillman, *Blue Fire*, Harper and Row, New York, 1989, pp.52-70.

The Theatre of Paralysis
Jon Thompson

STELLA SANTACATTERINA

From its very beginning, the work of Jon Thompson has followed a trajectory that is both isolated and coherent. This continuity was and still is under the sign of the mirror, of art's reflection about itself. But, as we know, reflection on art is the only one capable of taking us to a varied and infinite play of significations: a continuous interrogation in the freedom of a visionary play.

Thompson's recent body of work, always presented through an elegant economy of material means, comprises large black-and-white photographs in which, with few exceptions, the artist has used his own body in an exaggerated and almost mannerist fashion. The artist constructs a *mise-en-scène* often drawn from the imaginary archive of art history, the religious and the theatrical, to give form to the real subject – which is art and its deepest mechanism. This operation is similar to that of Duchamp, who used his own body as an 'assisted ready-made'. The transformation of his own image is captured in the act of formalising through the photograph, which resembles the paralysis of the 'sculptural' object itself.

If life is always fragmentary, an accumulation and reservoir, the language of art, by contrast, is what transforms the fragment to totality, the ordinary to the exceptional. The tendency to totality, which belongs to the creative act, mobilises the most profound levels of the unconscious. To give form means to arrest that movement, to capture the totality, and at the same time to dwell in the language of art, which is not life. The work of art is not the dissolution of the object, but rather an exercise which takes form as a separate entity, rupturing the relationship with its own author.

Jon Thompson's work privileges the emblematic aspect of the sign, the internal mechanisms of representation. Representation resolves itself in the theatre of paralysis: the big subjects like those of Eros, cruelty and death, are brought to the point where the Lacanian *ça parle* really means self-conjugation, in which everything is completely displaced within the realm of the signifier – because the work of art is always a formalisation that tends to condense time in exemplary space, a linguistic system displaced from the quotidian to a different temporality. For this reason, Derrida says that to speak is to know that thought must become a stranger to itself in order to manifest itself. This means that it must reclaim itself in the very moment it is given. Inspiration is also this.

Like Duchamp's *Door, 11 rue Larrey*, the body is a complex ready-made which holds a perverse familiarity,

recognisable and at the same time enigmatic. The body as matter is used and manipulated in a way typical of making art and sculpture, becoming, through the photographic procedure, the ultimate mould of an indestructible form. The theatre of paralysis is confirmed in the passage from the body-in-life as organic matter to the fixed and frozen form captured by the mechanical eye of the camera. As Blanchot says, "photography suspends death". This process constitutes a transference to immortality, where any gesture is definitive, no longer susceptible to further elaboration. From now on, matter, desire, the indefinable magma of impulses, find their own indestructible form.

This seems to be explicit in the series of works called *The Ultimate Act of Modelling*, which includes a photographic image in which the body of the artist assumes a position corresponding to that of St. Sebastian, similar but different to the familiar one in art history. Here the body is enveloped in a simple garment, like a protective membrane, which intercepts the path of the arrows of martyrdom. Martyrdom becomes the sculpture: the martyrdom of matter ascends to the sanctity of form. The structure of the sculpture is asymmetrical, bulky in the trunk, but tapering to the legs which acquire a female aspect, or better, an androgynous one. Thus the form of art resembles the neutral condition within which the Saint is generally represented.

In Thompson's image, the head is privileged over the body, assuming a position reminiscent of Rodin's *Thinker*. The overall expression of the sculpture takes the definitive form of a sacrificial offering. It is a sacrifice which does not conceal the necessity of form, or the elegance of the gesture, but declares sorrow through the presence of the arrows, pointing inwardly towards biological life. This life becomes conjugated in the paralysis of form, and crossed by plastic language which helps the pose to find the code to the ultimate *mise-en-pose*. The work now condenses a total temporality, from the beginning of life to the finality of death – terms which belong also to the destiny of humankind. In the photographic image of St. Sebastian, there is no appearance of deteriorating flesh, but rather the pulp skeleton of an essential language, durable in time. The temporal condition is, in fact, what depersonalises language, and makes possible the fixing of an image in a place which belongs to no one and excludes any biography or metaphor.

The images of the artist's body are images of art; they never assume an emblematic stasis or the dogmatic value of the artist's model. On the contrary, they present themselves as a lapsus, or a chance event from nowhere, which coincides with a fullness guaranteed by the possession of language over the world. Duchamp was the first to understand that the world cannot be replicated and that art in particular can no longer interpret or change the world, but can only reinvent it (or reduce it to zero) in a manner specific or peculiar to the mechanism of language. We can revisit the notion of contemporary art from Duchamp's work through the Lacanian idea of the Real – the obscure knot which is not even accessible through language, where thought stops, incapable of satisfactory elaboration. Jon Thompson's work becomes an attempt to represent the 'Real', in the sense of assuming the attitude of no longer constructing a model of the world but an alternative, giving voice to that as yet unexplored zone; and language is the only sharp weapon that the artist has to hand.

In another image from the series *The Ultimate Act of Modelling*, the artist built an architecture where once again his body is put to work in a *mise-en-pose*. The image carries a figure completely fixed in its own sculptural volume and gravity, where the pose presents another alternative to the face of the pure biology of life. This construction is not a simplistic antimony between life and death, but rather the two terms are put in a dialectic confrontation and are reinvented. The artist is fully aware that life means representation of the process of death – and death is the spectacle of life. As Georges Bataille reminds us, nothing is less animal than fiction, less or more distant from the real, from death.

The face and neck of the artist, framed by a blonde wig, are 'dis-figured' by fairly evenly distributed adhesive black dots, referring to holes in the skin. The 'hole' symbolises the real that opens into language. Thus the face becomes a mask, and therefore a sculpture, which is aware of the specularity of the photograph's image. What come to mind are the masks of Artaud's *Theatre of Cruelty*, or Japanese kabuki, where death and cruelty exude an eroticism stronger than eroticism itself, at the same time becoming signs. Here they are transformed by the rigour of the pose and captured in the coldness of the photograph's image. So the face becomes other, and what remains is symmetrical but not identical; or better, the other given through the face is language itself. As Derrida says (in *Writing and Difference*), "Because the face presents the other without metaphor, the word must not only translate thought, but it is necessary also that the body remains

language." In this *mise-en-scène* the face is transformed into female, but this is not a sign of loss of identity, but rather a recognition of the mirage of the language of art, which is never specular but substitutive. "I have more than one face, and I don't know which one mocks the other." (Bataille)

In an anal-emotive way, the work seeks to create the body of art: subjectivity gives way to impersonality, not in the sense that it would disappear (which would be impossible) but rather that it assumes the cold declination of an impersonal state, inside which there no longer exists the traditional relationship between subject and object. As Artaud said, "The work of art, or better, the artistic gesture, is born from an immediate gratuitousness that induces an act which is deprived of any benefit for the present." "The peculiarity of art is a cruelty which challenges divine creative gratuity." This connects with an earlier series, *Cruelty of the Classical Canon*, where the artist makes use of the tradition of the *vanitas*, which speaks of art as a gratuitous act. Thus, the strategy of the artist moves from a consciousness of death, sensing that any personal commitment is irrelevant. The impersonality (of the language of art) delays death and is extracted from the timid place of subjectivity.

The omnipotence of language repairs the impotence of life; the double of the image rescues and transforms the inert impracticability of the real. Like Duchamp, Thompson's work underlines the importance of detachment, because the world is a stage. Being is a theatrical condition. Being therefore acts as a character not as an organic thing with a specific location in which the fundamental destiny is to be born, mature and die. The subject of representation is a dramatic effect born from the scene of representation itself.

Part of a related body of work consists of an image of the artist's body, curled in a foetal-like position and entirely swathed in a semi-transparent fabric that twists into an umbilicus across the floor. This image draws on the concept of the auto-genesis of form and the dynamic of the creative process. Again, auto-genesis reminds us of Artaud's rebellion against the idea of being born from human coupling: "I am," he insisted, "born from my work." Another of Thompson's works, *Subject to the Gaze*, is a photograph of Bronzino's self portrait, under which the artist has had printed, "With a troubled brow and a breast moistened with smoke, you take away our sight – adorable thief – making yourself invisible, the better to steal from us the passage of time… : a vacant address."

UNTITLED

UNTITLED

UNTITLED

Melanie and her Mother
Melanie Manchot

AMANDA HOPKINSON

The French, predictably, have a phrase for it. "Until the age of forty, you have the face God gave you. From the age of 40 onwards, you have the face you gave yourself." The giant portraits of Melanie Manchot's mother are taken down from their prominent position in the winter winds above South Kensington tube station in London, and down from the walls of Zelda Cheatle's Mayfair gallery, and now stand propped at irregular intervals around the walls of Melanie's cavernous and glacial Brick Lane studio. Curiously, the sitter's expression appears to alter with every move: fair proof, if any were required, that it is the relationship of the gaze between the subject and viewer that determines how we respond to a given image. And that distance, actual or assumed, has much to do with it. In close-up, they are distinctly unnerving.

The more-than-lifesized portraits are about to find their next temporary homes. First at the Hales Gallery in East London, then simultaneously at the Edition Lutz Fiebig in Berlin and the Warehouse in Geneva. All the more appropriate, then, that in the most recent ones Frau Manchot is increasingly personalised, is more than ever ready to look you in the eye, and that the background is early morning light over the Swiss Alps. She has also moved from black-and-white into colour.

The images' scale and squareness already gives them a billboard quality. And they have, in any case, been displayed as billboards. Radio 4 checked public reactions both for the *Today* and *PM* programmes. Two lots of rush-hour commuters sparing a glance and a comment. The responses anticipated the one solicited by 'that' advert for Help the Aged. Fifty-something Pearl Read, posed like Eva Herzogovina modelling a Wonderbra, over the slogan: "The first thing you notice about her is her age". They were right, Radio 4's female interviewees were either embarrassed or perplexed, the men sneering and snickering: "There are magazines for guys who go for old women like that, but they sell a hell of a lot less than the ones with proper nudes in?" What is a 'proper' nude? Presumably a Barbie lookalike, legs to the armpits and silicone breast implants, flesh with the smooth sheen guaranteed only by plastic. A studio discussion is set up, between a former *Cosmo* editor and a porn publisher. It does not appear odd to the programme producers to be re-inforcing the mono-concept of women as consumers, as consumable, as aspiringly or necessarily glamorous. Or else they're not even trying to be 'proper' women and certainly have no right to be treated as 'proper' nudes. Pearl Read fared better. By sitting on the margins, her

body signifying her options between promoting a breast cancer awareness campaign and a respectable (if possibly destitute) old age, she is beginning to make a niche for herself in the older-woman stakes. Pearl Read is around 15 years Frau Manchot's junior, yet age alone is the defining feature.

So how do we, the gallery-goers, respond to the soft folds of a 67-year old's flesh, the transformations wrought by time on a body that, biologically, has accomplished its birthing and nurturing function? Melanie is her mother's only child; her father died suddenly when she was only three months old. Frau Manchot brought her up alone working as a bank clerk, until Melanie reached the age of 18 and left home for university (to study philosophy not photography). That was when her mother met her future husband, some 20 years ago. His first response, on seeing his wife's nudity displayed in public spaces in 1995, was "that is something private, for my eyes alone, and not for hundreds of people to walk in and gawp at". Yet his relationship with the portraits has changed drastically, accelerating over the last year. Instead his increasing closeness to the portraits parallels that with his wife. So the separation between sign and signifier has been accomplished.

That notion of violated privacy is presumably what the women passers-by found 'embarrassing'; that and their own difficulty in articulating their reactions. There are, after all, few but pejorative terms for the sags and flab, the wrinkles and inelasticity that cause so much of our flesh – starting with our breasts – to follow gravity, in the words of Dilly Keane, "on that long journey south from which there is no return". It is a predicament that Melanie's mother could hardly be oblivious to, and there was a compromise by which both her head and legs were cut from the earlier images. It was as though by truncating her mother, by excluding the parts that anyone familiar with her could recognise, Melanie would simultaneously depersonalise her and reveal what was most intensely personal and intimate about her.

These earlier images are also those more complex in creation, the negatives being transferred onto canvases treated with sand, pigmentation and primer. Once applied, the canvas was again brushstroked with silver gelatin (to make it light-sensitive, as in early photographic processes) before being developed and fixed (like modern black-and-white prints). Melanie then etched the distressed linen with graphite and charcoal, before finally streaking it with paint. She thus incorporated formal 'artistic' techniques she first utilised as a postgraduate at the Royal College of Art – she was in the same intake as Nick Waplington and David Hiscock, and now teaches there – while building on photography's first-established strength, portraiture, reliant for its successes upon veracity rather than artistry. Only in this instance, creases in the canvas intensify the effects of the folded flesh. And yet, the reviewer looking critically at the work on the gallery walls, exclaiming: "But this is like Whistler's portrait of his mother!" has also struck a point of reference. Ask for Melanie's own, and she prefers early Cindy Sherman to an American painter – but then cites the German Romantic Caspar David Friedrich, whose mysterious snowy mountain peaks are certainly reminiscent of those in her latest photographs. These have a sharper effect that the earlier series, in which smudges and lines cross-hatch the texture of skin. Here there is a clarity highlighted by the late dawn sharpness of contrast in the side-lit frames.

There are fifteen portraits in all, mostly of the upper torso, shot on a 5" x 4" camera and enlarged to 120 x 95 cms without losing any of the original definition. Both subject and photographer seem to have settled into feeling more comfortable with a slight upward tilt to the camera, and Frau Manchot is herself visibly more at ease with the process than five years ago. Rather than looking somewhat shyly down or askance, or else assuming a deliberately haughty pose, Frau Manchot is clearly focussed – looking at something out of frame when not engaging the viewer's gaze.

Melanie was herself upset by some of the responses to her work. Not by those in the Zelda Cheatle Gallery's visitors' book – which were lucid when critical, fulsome when complimentary, but by "the kind of negative public reaction to the posters, calling my mother an undesirable and fat old bag". Discussions between mother and daughter, as those between mother and stepfather, only brought the family closer as the necessity to disassociate the individuality of the sitter from her perceived status intensified. "By the end of it all, my mother was really wondering what the portraits actually contained of herself." The postmodern answer, presumably, is nothing since they only contain her portrait, a far cry from an earlier age of photo-portraiture which claimed to reveal the 'essence of the inner in the appearance of the outer man'.

To Frau Manchot, this is by now only grist to the mill of discourse. No longer moved by how she appears or how much she reveals, she has even a sense of standing in for her absent family, or for a whole community. The discussion has to address real (or perceived) issues rather

than personalities. Still game to carry on, even after an intensive period of collaboration while, for three years, Melanie worked on little else, it is Melanie who is now slowing down. Following a period of photographing her mother with her own daughter, Billie, Melanie is moving back into self-portraiture. Here intellectual discourse has clearly won out over creative impetus, by definition less thoughtful. The Madonna-like portraits of naked grand-mother and infant, which include one of 'breastfeeding' have been jettisoned primarily because Melanie does not feel right about using Billie's image without her consent. Just as Sally Mann does much to undermine her own credibility in obsessively documenting her children by admitting she has no memories of her own childhood so, by contrast, Melanie Manchot evinces respect in refusing to use her own infant as raw material for her art. The works, by common mother-daughter consent, will remain unexhibited (at least until the grand-daughter is grown), and no more will be made.

But it is the new series of portraits of her mother that is the major series in Melanie's next volume, *Vile Bodies*, due to be published late next year. Once again, the book is intended as a critical evaluation – in Melanie's terms: "It has to be issues – rather than work-based." It will appear in a similar format to the earlier *Look at You, Look at Me* (Friedrich Reinhardt Verlag, 1998) with essays by Katja Blomberg and Val Williams, and additional excerpts from the writings of John Berger. Her proximity to her mother, as a consequence of the increasingly collaborative nature of their work together, means that she will continue as intrinsic a theme to Melanie's work as her own self.

The return to self-portraiture as the other element in the book forms a loop and a contrast to the pregnancy Melanie documented so meticulously for 36 weeks. That double entity was there measured and studied, not as in medical records but more as in the documentation of some strange and exotic creature, like a sea-horse. Now that the hidden element, Billie, is over 18 months old, but "still too young to say no" – she is excluded from all but family snapshots: "The rest is too difficult and disturbing, there's a sexual element in child photography that too often goes unacknowledged. It's a conceptual problem I haven't yet resolved." The three generations of women in Melanie Manchot's family make not only powerfully haunting and loving portraits but also act as a reminder of how we are all more than either the division or the sum of any successive number of parts.

PORTRAIT OF MRS MANCHOT, 1997

BODY STUDY XII, 1996

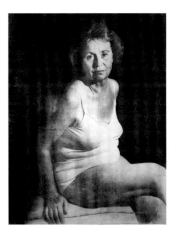

MRS MANCHOT WITH MOUNTAINS II, 1999

FORTHCOMING EXHIBITIONS OF
Photography
1999

John Coplans: A Self Portrait 1984 - 1997

THE DEAN GALLERY
29 MAY – 25 JULY 1999
Admission £1.50, Concessions £1.00

Murray Johnston's Landscapes

SCOTTISH NATIONAL PORTRAIT GALLERY
11 JUNE – 5 SEPTEMBER 1999
Admission Free

Caroline Rye: The Turin Machine

SCOTTISH NATIONAL PORTRAIT GALLERY
10 SEPTEMBER – 19 SEPTEMBER 1999
Admission Free

Magna Brava: The Magnum Women Photographers

SCOTTISH NATIONAL PORTRAIT GALLERY
5 November 1999 – 30 January 2000
Admission £2.50, Concessions £1.50
Sponsored by Burness Solicitors

National Galleries of Scotland

Edinburgh

For Further Information Telephone 0131 - 624 6200

Glasgow School of Art

School of Fine Art Degree Show

Glasgow School of Art
167 Renfrew Street Glasgow G3 6RQ tel 0141 353 4562

Private View
Friday 25 June 1999 6 - 9pm

Open to Public
Saturday 26 June - Friday 2 July 1999

Saturday 9.30am - 5pm Sunday 2 - 5pm
Monday - Thursday 9.30am - 8.30pm
Friday 9.30am - 5pm

Master of Fine Art Show

McLellan Galleries
270 Sauchiehall Street Glasgow tel 0141 331 1854

Private View
Friday 25 June 1999 6-9pm

Open to Public
Saturday 26 June - Saturday 10 July 1999

Daily 10am - 6pm Thursday 10am -8pm
Sunday 11am - 6pm

Edinburgh COLLEGE of ART

HERIOT-WATT UNIVERSITY

DEGREE SHOWS 1999

FACULTY OF ART & DESIGN

12 - 22 June 1999

Mon - Thur 10am - 8pm
Fri Sat Sun 10am - 5pm

FACULTY OF ENVIRONMENTAL STUDIES

19 - 28 June 1999

Mon - Thur 10am - 8pm
Fri Sat Sun 10am - 5pm

For further information please contact
Diane Henderson
Edinburgh College of Art
Lauriston Place
Edinburgh
Tel 0131 221 6032
E-mail d.henderson@eca.ac.uk

portfolio

the catalogue of contemporary photography in britain

PORTFOLIO is the best way to keep informed about the most innovative photographic art created and shown in Britain. Published in June and December each year, PORTFOLIO combines the contemporary interests and current reviews of a magazine with the quality reproductions and detailed information of an exhibition catalogue. Past issues of PORTFOLIO have featured the work of established photographic artists with in-depth essays and lively reviews from esteemed writers and curators. Back issues can be obtained individually or in a money-saving set of the ten most recent catalogues.

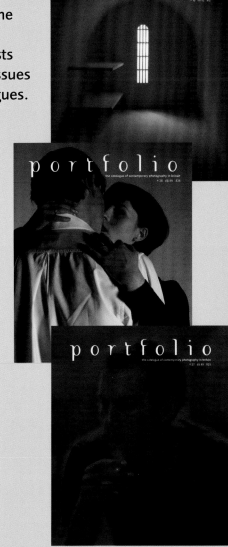

back issues

Issue 22
Paul Graham
Allan Sekula
Joel-Peter Witkin
Martin Parr
Pavel Büchler
Helen Sear
Wendy McMurdo
Lucinda Devlin
Dorte Eisfeldt
Ann Mandelbaum

Issue 21
Andres Serrano
Helen Chadwick
Olivier Richon
Zarina Bhimji
Catherine Yass
Roger Palmer
Andrea Fisher
Hannah Collins

Issue 20
Yve Lomax
David Williams
Thomas Joshua
Cooper
Mari Mahr
David Hiscock
Lynn Silverman
Lesley Punton
Roddy Buchanan

Issue 19
Maud Sulter
Boyd Webb
Susan Trangmar
Karen Knorr
Calum Angus Mackay
John Stathatos
Anne Rome Elliot
Catriona Grant

Issue 24
Calum Colvin
Gabriel Orozco
John Goto
Susan Trangmar
Willie Doherty
Richard Billingham
Robert Mapplethorpe
Jim Mooney
Annette Heyer

Issue 23
Helen Chadwick
Jeff Wall
Susan Hiller
Keith Piper
Orlan
Clare Strand
Liz Rideal
Katrina Lithgow
Jim Harold
Clement Cooper

Issue 26
Avi Holtzman
Rut Blees Luxemburg
David Griffiths
Britta Jaschinski
Jim Harold
Bridget Smith
Owen Logan
Robin Dance
James Morris
Torsten Lauschman

Issue 25
Mat Collishaw
Catherine Yass
Karen Knorr
Hannah Collins
Evergon
Roger Palmer
Anthony Haughey
Lynn Silverman
Peter Lavery
John Darwell
Anne Bjerge Hansen

Issue 28
Sharon Kivland
Sophie Calle
Joy Gregory
Jorges Molder
Yinka Shonibare
Zarina Bhimji
Tracey Moffatt
Robin Gillanders
Bryndis Snæbjörnsdóttir
Kate Mellor
Detlef Henrichs

Issue 27
Paul Graham
Rineke Dikjstra
Marie-Jo Lafontaine
Joan Fontcuberta
Gabriele Basilico
Hiroshi Sugimoto
Jorma Puranen
Abigail Lane
Karen Ingham
Suky Best
Jago Brown

Native Nations
Barbican Art Gallery, London

JOHN STATHATOS

A TEWA GIRL
Edward S. Curtis

Native Nations, subtitled 'Journeys in American Photography', was an ambitious exploration of the photographic representation of Native American Indians. A collaboration between the Barbican and the Smithsonian's National Anthropological Archives, it was divided into two parts, uneven in size and quality, which reflected the ideological and aesthetic issues besetting this thorny subject. The first part dealt with 19th century images taken by whites, while the second concentrated on Native American photographers and artists documenting their own communities. The work of 20th century white photographers such as Laura Gilpin was excluded, an absence which, while under-standable in the context of the exhibition's underlying discourse, still left a gap in the record.

Part one was by far the most powerful; it was also an eloquent demonstration of the way representational photography echoes power relationships between depicter and depicted. This was made clear by such works as Benjamin Franklin Upton's grim stereographs of captive warriors, George Trager's brutally casual photo of Chief Big Foot lying dead in the snow at Wounded Knee, and, above all, John Nicholas Choate's photographs of Native American children at the infamous Carlisle School, particularly the before-and-after pairings contrasting children in native dress with their 'civilised' makeover after they had been shorn, cowed and uniformed. The Carlisle experiment, with its dedication to the principle that one must "kill the Indian in order to save the man", seems particularly chilling today.

Inevitably dominating this section were the dramatic images of Edward S. Curtis, of whom James C. Faris has written in irritated admiration that "[he] hangs like a stone around the neck of the photography of Native Americans". There is ample evidence that Curtis staged many of his images, often using wildly inappropriate props, and that his approach was characterised by the sentimental nostalgia appropriate to a defeated and romanticised 'noble savage'. Nevertheless, Curtis's vision permeated the exhibition in more ways than one; *The Three Scouts* (1908), a key image by Richard Throssel, the earliest Native American to feature in part two, could easily be mistaken for a particularly fine Curtis, with its

Crow warriors on horseback standing among tombstones, rifles raised against a brooding sky.

That only two Native American photographers active at the turn of the century should have been discovered (the other was the remarkable Jenny Ross Cobb) is hardly surprising; as Hulleah Tsinhnahjinnie dryly remarks in a catalogue essay, "The focus of my relatives was the reality of survival, keeping one's family alive. Time to contemplate Western philosophy or the invention of photography was, shall we say, limited." Tsinhnahjinnie's essay is one of four 'photographic journeys' by contemporary Native American photographers seeking to reclaim representation of their people – an issue which begs the question of the extent to which photographs of a society by insiders differ from those taken by outsiders, and which inevitably leads to the more basic argument of whether there is any such thing as inherent traits in the photography of a particular group, people or nation.

In terms of accuracy and sympathy, the answer is obviously that it makes a very considerable difference. The scientific value of traditional anthropological photography has been successfully challenged by anthropologists such as Elisabeth Edwards and James C. Faris; indeed Faris, in his magisterial study *Navajo and Photography*, has demonstrated the often ludicrous ways in which so-called scientific photography inevitably falsified or misinterpreted data, or

distorted it in the light of racial and cultural prejudice. In the area of documentary photography, therefore, the work of Native American photographers such as Throssel, Horace Poolaw and Dugan Aguilar undoubtedly breaks new, if mostly unspectacular, ground.

Whereas the documentary photography of insiders is often superior to that of outsiders in terms of fidelity and perception, it is far from evident that there are significant differences one way or another where aesthetics are concerned. Certainly the final group of works by contemporary Native Americans fine artists proved a distinct disappointment. Shelley Niro's role-playing self-portraits, Larry McNeil's poetic text and image prints evoking Indian legends and Jolene Rickard's CD-ROM installation all demonstrated considerable sophistication and an evident familiarity with contemporary artistic discourse. Unfortunately, they were also characteristic of that vast body of artistic production generated by and within the American academic establishment: serious, informed and well-mannered, it is also by and large sterile and uninvolving. None of these examples really succeeded in rising above their institutional background, making for an unexpectedly subdued ending to an otherwise passionate and intelligent exhibition.

Secret Victorians
Hayward Gallery National Touring Exhibition

JOANNA LOWRY

The pretext for this exhibition is that a Victorian sensibility is alive and well in contemporary culture and that it makes sense to look again at some of those practices that we have become used to characterising as 'post-modern' and to recognise their affinity to, and indeed continuity with, cultural practices that pre-dated modernism. Taking their inspiration from recent re-evaluations of the Victorian period by historians like Steven Marcus and Peter Gay that have emphasised its spirit of 'eccentricity, ingenuity and complexity', the selectors have trawled the practices of contemporary fine art for the decorative, the eccentric, the experimental and the metaphysical, and developed an exhibition which is both fascinating and slightly mad. Under a series of thematic headings: Ornament and Sexuality, Collecting and Colonialism, Science and Crime, Photography and Death, they have collected the work of an eclectic group of painters, sculptors and photographers whose work might otherwise occupy very different spaces. In a way the project that they have undertaken is perhaps less spurious and superficial with respect to photography than it is with respect to painting and sculpture, where it seems to me that the terrain has really shifted too much during the last century to claim anything more than an ironic or parodic relationship to the past. In the case of photography, however, we have a different situation.

One of the consequences

WORLD'S EXPOSITION, 1997
Kara Walker

of the recent explosion of photographic activity by contemporary fine artists has been the marginalisation of a particular modernist trajectory within photography and a return to a much more open and fluid set of discourses arising out of an experimentation with the technology itself. Artists have forced us to look again at the photographic image as the product of a series of particular apparatuses and processes. They have plundered aspects of photographic practice – the scientific, the popular, and the mystical – that had hitherto been considered marginal to the development of photography as a properly modernist art. This has coincided with a revived interest by theorists and historians in the 19th century as the source of an alternative history of photography, one which might emphasise the spectacular, the magical, the mystical and the

theatrical, rather than the documentary quest for the real. This in its turn has led to a new interest in early forms of photography such as the combination print, scientific records, spirit photography, the stereograph, and popular masquerade, which had more usually been seen as eccentric diversions from the onward march of the medium into modernity. If at one level we can see *Secret Victorians* as representing a kind of protest against the dictates of modernism and an evocation of Victorian sensibility as a kind of return of the repressed, then it seems particularly appropriate to the current re-evaluations of the medium that are taking place within the discipline.

Artists like Steven Pippin, making a pinhole camera out of the toilet-bowl in a railway carriage, or Matt Collishaw, adapting an old large-format wooden camera so that the

ephemeral elusive image of moving waterfall can play across its viewfinder, or Douglas Gordon, re-looping found footage from the medical archives of the First World War, are clearly all in their separate ways engaged with a continuation of a peculiarly 19th century fascination with, and fetishisation of, the machine. Helen Chadwick's use of photographs of embryonic cells and Laura Stein's glossy photographic records of her macabre grafting experiments with plants each consciously exploit the history of the scientific record. Sally Mann, whose compelling theatrical tableaux of a dangerous and idyllic childhood often make explicit reference to the photographs of Julia Margaret Cameron, can be seen as representing the female Victorian amateur, troubling the mainstream with her evocations of a strangely ambivalent domestic world.

Some of the connections made by this exhibition are perhaps tendentious and arbitrary: we are sometimes asked to stretch the initial premise too far and to incorporate too many diverse practices into the Victorian frame. However it is also certainly clear that, at the end of the century, photography no longer bears the burden of representing progress and modernity. As the technology of photography is forced to confront its own potential obsolescence, we are all re-viewing its history and identity in a new light. *Secret Victorians* does offer some insights into the form that such a re-evaluation might take.

Common Sense: Photographs by Martin Parr
Dewi Lewis Publishing

MARK DURDEN

There is no room for words in this book: from front cover to back cover we get full colour images. The cover gives a close up of a globe of the world, used for the collection of money. It's a cue for the orgy of world consumption which Martin Parr pictures in detail throughout this book: money makes the world go around. Only Parr's globe has passed its use-by date; it is worn and rusty. And his picturing of an orgy of consumption is coupled with an entropic sense of waste and decay. Interrupting all the pictures of people stuffing their faces, are certain abject details: a sticky lollipop dropped on the floor, a putrefying banana, a degraded bar code, a bruised apple. It's not all perfect goods.

This is by far Parr's most savagely witty and brilliant book to date. It offers up a glut of pictures, a brutal and comic display of a worldwide consumerist frenzy. The colour photos offer details and close-ups of half-eaten food, of hands stuffing mouths with sweets, ice creams, burgers, popcorn and meats. It's a world of excess and indulgence conveyed through a glut of over-the-top images. The very excesses of Parr's pictures perfectly accord with the excesses of consumption shown: viewing this book, we too are engorged, sated, have more than our fill.

What is distinctive is the visceral impact of so many images. The selective focus of the close up detail heightens our sense of the physicality and presence of things, which offsets and plays against the recurring

UNTITLED (Courtesy Magnum)

emphasis on decoration. Parr makes substantial the very things which ordinarily speak to us of surface illusion, glitter and fakery: all the painted toes and finger nails, the fancy hairdos, the toys, the fancy cakes, the hilarious dolled-up dogs. The saturated colour is comparable to sunburn: made explicit in the brutal pairing of a male chest burning on the beach with vivid red meat hanging on hooks in a butcher's stall. Parr's world is also one of innuendo and puns, there are elements of saucy postcard humour here – phallic plastic bananas paired with hollow ice-cream cones and Parr's variant on the advertising trope of food and fellatio as half-eaten foodstuff is paired with the open mouth of a blow up doll.

The pictures were taken in every continent of the world and the launch of the book was celebrated by simultaneous exhibitions in more than 30 different cities worldwide. It's

very much a global view. And while some images clearly invite national stereotypes – from Germany's periscope-shaped salami and shaven skinhead to an abundance of signifiers for Englishness: a cup of tea, Brussels sprouts, wasps in jam, the tattooed lager lout – difference is subsumed by the overriding uniform, repetitive act of consumption. It is in this respect one understands the full significance of the book's title: that the common sense is the sense we have in common, a base sense of greedy over-consumption.

Bad taste is integral to this book. Parr continues his love of kitsch. He revels in kitsch and in so doing takes it to new surreal realms and intensities. Unlike his previous books and projects, Parr mostly avoids giving us identifiable pictures of people. He goes in so close we only see the consumers through formally compelling fragmentary details, bits of faces: a freshly lipsticked

smile, a $100 dollar bill hanging out of a woman's mouth. Instead of human faces and expressions we have only the stunned gaping or blank stares of mannequins and dolls. Such hollow signs for subjectivity underscore the lack of social interaction and subjectivity in Parr's world view. This social distance, which has always remained the problematic core of documentary practice, gives a distinctive misanthropic cast to the whole book.

A number of details show switches, dials and buttons, suggesting the mechanical activity of consumption, the quick click of a consumerist take. Photography is of course associated with this, and Parr seems to acknowledge this with an opening shot showing a Japanese snapshooter. And in doing so, he allows for the possibility that his own relentless photographing could be seen to parallel the compulsive consumption so vividly and brilliantly brought out in this book. While he erases the potential for any social interaction and the often cruel and objectifying nature of his documentary practice continues, he does at least suggest that he too can never really remain outside this global consumer frenzy.

Common Sense – Photographs by Martin Parr, Dewi Lewis Publishing, £25.00. Hardback, 206mm x 300mm, 160 pages, 158 colour photographs, ISBN 1899235078.

Annelies Strba
The Photographers' Gallery, London

SIMON MORRISSEY

For over 20 years Annelies Strba has concentrated almost exclusively on documenting the evolution of her family, especially her two daughters Sonja and Linda, following them from infancy through to adulthood. This continual and intensely personal subject, with its accompanying association that Strba is documenting something she is firmly within rather than apart from, locates her project in a similar territory to that of more prominent artists such as Nan Goldin or Richard Billingham. Although the tenor of Strba's work is more meditative than that of either Goldin or Billingham, it could be argued that together with them she has attempted to undermine the implicit hierarchy between artist and subject through an attempt to create photographs out of relationships, not observation, with all the complication that that entails.

Despite the power of many of Strba's single images, the natural orientation and real strength of her work is cumulative. Although the artist also exhibits her images as prints, their interdependence is most accurately represented in a form that encourages the consumption and cross-association of a flood of the images in quick succession. This is achieved in Strba's book *Shades of Time,* and the way that the work was realised for The Photographers' Gallery – projected simultaneously on three carousel projectors – is the closest the artist has come to emulating this in an exhibition.

The images appear and

LINDA AND OMAR, 1994

dissolve and, as they do, an affectionate yet complex portrait of her family slowly evolves. Strba's offspring are seen as children, later as adolescents, then as young adults with children of their own. The wealth of images of her family are juxtaposed against blurred and often distorted landscapes or fragments of cityscapes. The often loaded cultural identities of these places (Chernobyl, Hiroshima, Kobe, Bronte country) are unacknowledged in the installation and thus have a generic anonymity – a fairy-tale castle on a hill, a power station bathed in golden light, cottages in the country, a sun-drenched park covered in a carpet of floral tributes – that cannot be more precisely fixed through the accumulation of detail as in the photographs of the family. In this way, the landscapes work as a sort of punctuation to the relentless portrait of the family, a fleeting

web of a wider context that only works to intensify Strba's concentration on her familial relationships.

Through its continual catalogue of images, Strba's work appears to unfold an intimate, informal portrait of the artist's extended family in front of the viewer. The circumstantial aesthetic, the lack of obvious overt composition, the presence of flash-victim red-eye in her subjects, all testify to her use of basic tools and the immediacy of her execution in image-making. The portrayal of her subjects within a constant domestic environment, in various stages of undress, asleep or bathing, compound ideas of the unmediated record of activity that is still so strongly assumed to belong to photography, and in particular to projects such as Strba's.

Yet although Strba's work undoubtedly reveals the dynamic

between herself, her daughters, and her wider family, with an intimacy that can only come from being a part of the emotional landscape she is portraying, it would be disingenuous to argue that it is the dynamic of a normal family. Instead Strba's portrait is that of a family with an extreme consciousness of the camera's presence. It is evident in the work that living under the constant scrutiny of their mother's camera has made Sonja and Linda explicitly conscious of themselves, and of the potential for their private action to become public image. Within the portrayal of the seemingly idyllic post-hippy atmosphere of the Strba household, there is always an uncommon level of awareness in the daughters' faces of their position as 'subject' – as beings subjected to constant scrutiny and subsequent display.

Although their attitude towards this fluctuates between acceptance and confrontation, willingness and evasion, surprisingly it is a constant presence even in the photographs of them as young children. And thus, despite the obvious definition of Strba's work as a mediation on the family, ultimately the real compulsion of her work lies in a more elusive relationship – that of the continual competition between photographer and subject for control of the image.

Koudelka in Wales
Cardiff

PAUL RYAN

Josef Koudelka's images call to mind that section on the French television news where a few minutes of film footage are shown without a reporter's commentary. This segment is given an English title which might be applied to Koudelka's work: No Comment. Koudelka, even more than the French news team, puts the onus on the viewer to draw conclusions. Take his haunting photograph of a deserted Prague street in August 1968. In the bottom foreground is an arm, extending half-way across the frame, bearing a wristwatch which shows the time as 12.20. The title gives us nothing but the place and date, but we can extrapolate the rest from the emptiness of the street and the tense impatience of that arm. A demonstration against the Russian invasion was due to take place at 12 noon but the population, fearful of reprisals, stayed away. The force of the composition takes you beyond explanations, it takes you into the moment and holds you there for as long as you can bear to look.

This was part the famous series, *Prague 68* with which Koudelka first made his reputation, if not quite his name (until 1984 the shots were attributed to "an unknown Czech photographer" to spare Koudelka and his family from official recrimination). Koudelka, the strictest of self-editors, will now show only twelve of the many photographs he took at the time of the invasion. At Turner House, Penarth, just outside of Cardiff, they were shown alongside Koudelka's *Theatre* images in one

FRANCE, 1987 (Courtesy Magnum)

of the four exhibitions which comprised *Koudelka in Wales*. Paradoxically, the starkly stylised theatre work provided some relief from the real drama of the Prague streets and highlighted the profound sense of theatre that runs through Koudelka's work.

Gesture, ritual and their traces are present in every image. Even when he plunges into the heart of a community, Koudelka does not shy away from loneliness, whether in human beings or in the landscapes which they inhabit. No matter how swift his eye, it produces images which hold the gaze for inordinate periods. A Koudelka photograph is an object of contemplation, possessed of an almost religious intensity, which evokes a uniquely personal response. This was evident at Cardiff's Ffotogallery where the unabridged version of the celebrated 1988 exhibition *Exiles* was presented. The true exile, of course, is Koudelka himself. In pluralising the title he

claims and invites comradeship with the people, animals and landscapes he encounters on his travels. Koudelka's images bear witness to endurance, human and otherwise. Are those Italian peasants or gypsies burying a young member of their family? Is the frugal meal, spread out on a copy of the Herald Tribune, Koudelka's own? Does the dog, arching its back in the French snow, have an owner? No Comment. Yet each image in *Exiles*, no matter how mysterious, lodges itself like a splinter in the mind.

Landscapes also suffer and endure, and the centrepiece of *Koudelka in Wales* is a collection of panoramic landscapes of South Wales, presented in two locations. *Contact* at the Cardiff Bay Arts Trust Gallery featured 60 panoramic contact prints which combined to portray the post-industrial life of an area which has been mined, exploited and inadequately healed by the agents

of progress. Sixteen large panoramics formed *Reconnaissance*, the inaugural exhibition at the new Art in Wales Gallery based at the National Museum of Wales (see pages 40 - 43). Several of these feature landscapes of my own childhood in the docks area of Cardiff, in particular the bleakly beautiful mudflats which are about to disappear beneath a hugely expensive freshwater marina. I may mourn the loss of an irreplaceable inter-tidal marsh and estuary complex which was home to thousands of migratory birds, also doomed; but to condemn an economically depressed community for surrendering its treasures, its identity, is the arrogance of exile. The unlovely, living waterfront is about to be usurped by the deadly picturesque and Koudelka has caught the soul of a disappearing landscape with terrible precision.

It was a brave initiative of Ffotogallery and the Cardiff Bay Arts Trust to invite Koudelka to make these images and to place them in the wider historical context of his earlier work. His response to the Welsh landscape reveals a commitment similar to that evident in his documentation of the devastated *Black Triangle* of Northern Bohemia. The resulting images are unsentimental and troubling in their refusal of convention, their unflinching acknowledgement of consequences. One day, Koudelka's panoramics of the mudflats may adorn the walls of the fine hotels and apartments that overlook Cardiff's bright new marina. No comment.